Devon
and Exmoor

AA Publishing

Authors: Penny Phenix and Paul Murphy

Walks: David Hancock

Page layout: Jo Tapper

Produced by AA Publishing
© Automobile Association Developments Ltd 1996, 1999, 2002.

Published by AA Publishing (a trading name of Automobile Association Developments Limited, whose registered office is Millstream, Maidenhead Road, Windsor, Berkshire, SL4 5GD. Registered Number 1878835)

First edition published 1996, reprinted 1996, 1997, 1998. Second edition 1999, reprinted November 1999 and September 2000 Third edition 2002.

Ordnance Survey® This product includes mapping data licensed from Ordnance Survey® with the permission of the Controller of Her Majesty's Stationery Office. © Crown copyright 2002. All rights reserved. Licence number 399221

Mapping produced by the Cartographic Department of The Automobile Association. A00691.

ISBN 07495 3293 9

A CIP catalogue record for this book is available from the British Library.

Gazetteer map references are taken from the National Grid and can be used in conjunction with Ordnance Survey maps and atlases. Places featured in this guide will not necessarily be found on the maps at the back of the book.

All the walks are on rights of way, permissive paths or on routes where de facto access for walkers is accepted. On routes which are not on legal rights of way, but where access for walkers is allowed by local agreements, no implication of a right of way is intended.

Visit the AA Publishing website at www.theAA.com

Colour reproduction by L C Repro

Printed and bound by G. Canale & C. s.p.a., Torino, Italy

Contents

Lynton

Ilfracombe

Lynmou

Combe
Martin

Woolacombe

Arlington

Braunton

Barnstaple

Nort
Molto

Fremington

Lundy

Barnstaple
or
Bideford Bay

Westward Ho!

Bideford

South
Molton

Hartland Point

Clovelly

Hartland

Great
Torrington

DEVON

Stibb Cross

Chawlei

Bradworthy

**DEVON'S RURAL
HEARTLAND**

Eggesford

Sheepwash

Winkleigh

Bude

Hatherleigh

Holsworthy

Northlew

North
Tawton

Okehampton

621m
High Willhays

**DARTMOOR
AND THE
TAMAR VALLEY**

Chagford

Launceston

Mary Tavy

Dartmoor

Mana

*Bodmin
Moor*

Princetown

Tavistock

Ashburt

Horrabridge

CORNWALL

Yelverton

Bodmin

Buckfastleigh

Liskeard

Saltash

Plympton

Lostwithiel

Torpoint

PLYMOUTH

Modbury

St Austell

Fowey

Looe

**THE ENGLIS
AND SOUT**

Newton
Ferrers

Whitsand Bay

Kingsbri

Bigbury-on-Sea

Bigbury Bay

Salcombe

0   20 km

0   10 miles

Minehead

Porlock

Exmoor

Dunster

monsbath

**EXMOOR AND
THE NORTH COAST**

Bridgwater Bay

Glastonbury

Bridgwater

Taunton

Bampton

Yeovil

Witheridge

River Exe

Blackdown
Hills

Tiverton

**EXETER
AND
EAST DEVON**

Crewkerne

Bickleigh

Cullompton

Chard

Cheriton
Fitzpaine

Silverton

Honiton

Axminster

DORSET

editon

Broadclyst

Ottery
St Mary

Colyton

River Axe

EXETER

Topsham

Branscombe

Seaton

Lyme
Regis

Bridport

Dunsford

etonhampstead

Exminster

Sidmouth

Beer

ovey
acey

Exmouth

Budleigh
Salterton

Lyme Bay

Newton
Abbot

Dawlish

Teignmouth

Kingskerswell

Babbacombe Bay

Totnes

■ **TORQUAY**

Paignton

Berry Head

well

9

Brixham

VIERA
AMS

Dartmouth

Slapton

Start Bay

Torcross

8

Start Point

Introducing Devon and Exmoor

Devon offers more variety than most counties in terms of landscape and holiday attractions. There are two National Parks for a start – Dartmoor and Exmoor – where beautiful and unique landscapes are being conserved. It has two coastlines, with long sandy beaches, rocky coves, daunting cliffs and pretty fishing villages. Even the resorts offer plenty of choice, depending on whether you want to sit in a deck chair or do some surfing – in Devon you can find the sophisticated, the sedate or traditional seaside fun.

Inland Devon is everyone's idea of a rural idyll, except, perhaps, those who are trying to make a living from the land. The patchwork of fields on steep hillsides is dotted with pretty thatch and cob villages and down-to-earth market towns. History is all around, particularly the maritime heritage that is so much a feature of Devon's two lively cities – Exeter and Plymouth.

THE OTTER
The tumbling streams of Devon are one of the last English strongholds of the shy otter

CHARLES KINGSLEY
Charles Kingsley evoked the West Country landscape of his youth in the well-loved novel Westward Ho! *(1855)*

WOOLACOMBE
Devon's sheltered coves and broad beaches offer a great setting for family holidays

SAND CROCUS
The unstable sand dunes at places such as Braunton Burrows shelter a distinctive flora

CREAM TEAS
Devon's famous clotted cream can be sampled in one (or more!) of the local, mouthwatering cream teas

A CANAL TRIP
Discover the scenic Grand Western Canal by horse-drawn narrow boat, or walk along the tow path

HARTLAND POINT
If remote beauty is what you seek, look no further than the wild headlands and cliffs along Devon's northern shore

SIR FRANCIS DRAKE
Sir Francis Drake is for ever associated with Plymouth Hoe where, in 1588, he calmly finished off his game of bowls before finishing off the Spanish Armada

BRANSCOMBE CHURCH
Devon's ecclesiastical buildings present a wealth of fascinating architecture and history

THE PILGRIM FATHERS
The Mayflower also set sail from Plymouth, carrying the Pilgrim Fathers to a new life in the Americas in 1620

ESSENTIAL DEVON AND EXMOOR

If you have little time and you want to sample the essence of Devon and Exmoor:

Drive across the western part of Dartmoor on the B3212 and B3357 for wide open moorland views, dotted with granite tors... **Take** a boat trip from Dartmouth up-river to Totnes, allowing time to stroll around the delightful streets of both towns... **Go** to Hatherleigh market on a Tuesday to savour the working life of rural Devon... **Treat** yourself to a clotted cream tea at the National Trust's Old Bakery at Branscombe, a perfectly preserved traditional bakery in one of Devon's prettiest villages... **Walk** along the coast path around Hartland Point, for spectacular coastal scenery... **Join** an escorted horse-ride down the deep combes of the beautiful and atmospheric Doone Valley... **Follow** in the footsteps of Sir Francis Drake and the Pilgrim Fathers in Plymouth's historic Barbican and The Hoe... **Sample** the excellent Devon seafood at The Carved Angel in Dartmouth.

RED DEER
Red deer thrive on Exmoor, and may be seen, and heard, in full bellow during the autumn rut

TOP TEN BEACHES

Oddicombe
Meadfoot
Broadsands
Ness Cove
Maidencombe
Elberry Cove
Torcross
Blackpool Sands
Saunton Sands
Woolacombe &
Putsborough

HONEY FARM
For a different farm experience, observe the bees labouring on the honey farm at South Molton, and taste the flavours on offer

DARTMOOR
The crags and tors of Dartmoor possess a special magic, drawing visitors back year after year

A Weekend in Devon: Day One

For many people a weekend break or a long weekend is a popular way of spending their leisure time.

These four pages offer a loosely planned itinerary designed to ensure that you make the most of your time and see and enjoy the very best the area has to offer.

Options for wet weather are given and places with gazetteer entries are in **bold**.

Friday Night

Stay at the Horn of Plenty, Gulworthy (3 miles/4.8km west of Tavistock on the A390), a fine Georgian house where you can enjoy splendid views across the Tamar valley to Bodmin Moor along with personal attention and wonderful food. Have your pre-dinner drinks before a blazing log fire in the winter, or in the garden under a vine-covered pergola during the warmer summer months.

Experience an exciting view of history at Morwellham Quay

Left, outside exhibits include the farm and stables and the waterwheel

Below, indoor attractions include a re-construction of the Assayer's office

Saturday Morning

Drive south via the B3257 to **Morwellham Quay**, a fascinating re-creation of a copper port in its heyday, with costumed actor/guides and lots to see and do.

The highlight of a visit is a trip on the old miners' railway which takes you deep underground into one of the mines, where tableaux and a commentary illustrate the life of the workers there. Above ground again, don't miss a stroll around the farmyard and the stables of the Shire horses.

Another wet day option in Plymouth is to visit Saltram House

Walk to the spectacular White Lady Waterfall deep in Lydford Gorge, right

Look out for the semi-wild Dartmoor ponies, below, as you cross the moors

Saturday Lunch

Drive up through **Tavistock** and on to Dartmoor to the Peter Tavy Inn at Peter Tavy. Fully restored with old flagstone floors and oak timbers, you can enjoy good food with views of the moor.

Wet-weather option
If it's raining spend the day in **Plymouth** *and get undercover in the hi-tech Plymouth Dome, the National Marine Aquarium or the Plymouth Gin Distillery.*

Saturday Afternoon

Drive northwest to walk off your lunch in the spectacular **Lydford Gorge**. Marvel at the dramatic Devil's Cauldron close to Lydford Bridge and the 90-foot (27-m) high White Lady Waterfall at the end of the Gorge. There are paths of various lengths, but the full walk is about 3½ miles (5.6km).

Saturday Night

Loop around the top of Dartmoor (no roads cross the wild northwestern part), then down through narrow lanes to spend the night at the Gidleigh Park Hotel, near Chagford – the best hotel and the best food in Devon; not for those travelling on a budget.

A Weekend in Devon: Day Two

Though it may be hard to tear yourself away from such a fine hotel, this is the day to explore the delightful little villages and lanes of eastern Dartmoor en route to one of the most impressive religious foundations in the country. After that, a scenic river cruise between two of Devon's most interesting old towns.

Sunday Morning

Drive through the famous villages of **Widecombe in the Moor** and **Buckland in the Moor** before continuing southwards to **Buckfastleigh**. **Buckfast Abbey** is the main attraction here, with its beautiful abbey church, constructed in the early part of the 20th century and worth visiting for the stained glass alone. The community of monks here are famous for their production of Buckfast Tonic Wine and for the honey from the Buckfast hives, so allow enough time to visit their shop before you leave.

Buckfastleigh is also the home of the **Buckfast Butterfly Farm** and **Otter Sanctuary**, which are both delightful, the butterfly farm particularly so on a chilly day because the large glasshouses are kept at a tropical temperature. Both of these attractions are situated just behind the station, which is the terminus of the **South Devon Railway**. As an alternative to driving on to Totnes for the afternoon, you could take a trip on one of their steam trains for seven scenic miles (11.2km) of the Dart Valley (be sure to check on times for the return trip).

Visit the 13th-century church at Buckland in the Moor, above

Take a ride from Buckfastleigh on the Primrose Line, left

Below, discover a tropical paradise at the Butterfly Farm

Explore the historic town of Totnes, right

Enjoy lunch beside the river, watching the world pass by, below

Spend time exploring old Dartmouth, right

Take to the water in Dartmouth, below, or return on the train

Sunday Lunch

Stop for lunch at the Waterman's Arms at Ashprington, south of Totnes. This famous old country inn has an interesting past – it has been a smithy, a brewhouse and even a prison during the Napoleonic War. Situated on the banks of the River Cart next to the Bow Bridge, which dates back to Domesday, the inn is full of character. The bars have exposed beams and open fires and offer an extensive snack menu with daily blackboard specials. The informal restaurant is separate from the bustling bars.

Sunday Afternoon

Wet-weather option
*If it is raining, go to **Exeter** and look round its wonderful **cathedral**, and visit the **Royal Albert Memorial Museum**. The **Underground Passages** are well protected from the elements.*

Take a boat trip down the beautiful River Dart from **Totnes** to **Dartmouth** and back. You will pass Greenway house on the way – the place where Agatha Christie wrote many of her novels.

Dartmouth's network of tiny little cobbled streets are delightful to explore and are a good place to indulge in a bout of window-shopping among the galleries, craft shops and boutiques. The historic quay at Bayard's Cove has hardly changed since the days of sail.

Totnes is an ancient town with some remarkably well-preserved buildings, more craft shops and galleries and one of the most attractive high streets in the country.

Exmoor and The North Coast

The north coast of Devon encompasses many changes in character from east to west. At its most easterly point, it is backed by Exmoor, with deep combes cutting their way down to the sea between steeply folded wooded slopes. West of the National Park are the traditional holiday resorts of Ilfracombe and Woolacombe and a series of long sandy beaches. Beyond Barnstaple and Bideford it changes again, with rocky foreshores which have to be approached steeply from above and delightful villages, such as Bucks Mills and Clovelly, perched above their harbours. The rocks continue around Hartland Point down to the lovely Welcombe beach.

APPLEDORE'S SEAFARING HERITAGE

Devon sailors have always been highly regarded and much sought after as crewmen, particularly in Elizabethan times when foreign parts – and foreign vessels – were considered ripe for the picking and great fortunes were to be made. Appledore men sailed with Drake to repel the Spanish Armada and such was their contribution that Elizabeth I rewarded the village by making it a free port, a privilege which still applies, meaning that there is no charge made on shipping using the harbour. Appledore's prosperous shipyard was the first in Britain to be nationalised.

Appledore's historic narrow lanes remain traffic-free

APPLEDORE   Map ref SS4630

Appledore's narrow cobbled streets, only just wide enough for a single car and lined with pretty colour-washed cottages, rise steeply up the hillside from the quay on the Torridge estuary. But, delightful though it certainly is, this is not simply a tourist village living on its appearance. Appledore is a lively community with a strong sense of its ancient maritime traditions, where shipbuilding and seafaring have occupied the workforce since medieval times.

Appropriately, Appledore is the home of the North

Devon Maritime Museum, in a listed building overlooking the village. Each room shows a different aspect of the maritime activities of the area, and there is a reconstruction of an Appledore kitchen at around the turn of the century. Visit the museum and then stroll around the village and along the quay to really soak up the atmosphere of the place.

ARLINGTON COURT   Map ref SS6140

There is no getting away from the fact that the exterior of Arlington Court is less than impressive. Indeed, it is plain, but don't judge this particular book by its cover, for inside are a series of rooms which are beautifully designed and furnished and which house a number of wonderful collections. Generations of the Chichester family have lived at Arlington, but today it reflects most of all the character of the last of them to live there – the remarkable and immensely energetic Miss Rosalie Chichester who bequeathed her home to the National Trust when she died in 1949. An intrepid traveller and compulsive collector, Miss Chichester filled the house with many and varied collections, including some 200 ship models, 75 cabinets full of shells, hundreds of pieces of pewter and snuff boxes and various ethnological items collected during her world travels. One of the nicest things about Arlington Court is the lack of barriers, enabling visitors to wander at will around each of the rooms, inspecting the contents at close quarters.

A pleasant walk through the grounds (see also Walk on page 14) leads to the superb stable block, which is a major attraction in itself. This is where the National Trust's collection of nearly 50 horse-drawn vehicles is kept, from enormous state carriages to a delightful little carriage built for a child in true fairy-tale fashion.

A PIONEER SAILOR
The name of Chichester and the preoccupation with ships and travel at Arlington Court may give a clue to another family connection. Sir Francis Chichester, the first person to sail single-handed round the world, was the nephew of Rosalie and was a frequent visitor to Arlington Court when he was a boy. The Ship Lobby contains a specially commissioned model of *Gypsy Moth IV*, the vessel in which he completed his epic voyage in 1967.

The landscape artist at Arlington Court planned views with care, including this glimpse of the little grey church across the still waters

Wooded Valleys Around Arlington Court

A peaceful ramble through National Trust woodland and across farmland paths around the wooded slopes of the Yeo Valley. It is well waymarked but many of the woodland paths can be wet and muddy in winter. Arlington Court (NT) is well worth a visit and the walk can be extended to incorporate the nature trail around the lake and parkland.

Time: 3 hours. Distance: 5¾ miles (9.3km).
Location: 5 miles (8km) northeast of Barnstaple.
Start: Arlington Court (NT) car park, half a mile (0.8km) off the A39. (OS grid ref: SS611408.)
OS Map: Outdoor Leisure 9 (Exmoor)
1:25,000
See Key to Walks on page 121.

ROUTE DIRECTIONS

From the car park follow the lane left into the hamlet of Arlington and bear right along a no through road towards the church. At the access track to the church keep left to pass National Trust buildings and follow waymarked route (blue arrow) along a concrete track. Shortly, bear right, then left on to an arrowed path through a copse to a gate.

Turn right along the field-edge track, pass through a waymarked wooden gate on the left in the field corner and follow a good path along the edge of trees before passing through two further gates (**Arlington Park and obelisk** visible to your right). Descend on a grassy path to a gate, pass through a copse and further gates and gently go downhill along a line of trees to a gate and enter Deerpark Wood.

Cross a brook, then at a crossing of tracks, keep ahead following the blue-arrowed route which soon ascends steeply through mainly coniferous trees, signed 'Loxhore Church', to reach a waymarked gate on the woodland fringe. Proceed across pasture towards a lone tree, go through a gate and join a hedged bridleway

The mansion of Arlington Court, built in 1822, is a veritable treasure-house

leading in to Loxhore.

Turn right along the lane passing South Town Farm to a T-junction, then turn right and descend steeply for a quarter of a mile (0.4km) into Loxhore Cott. Bear right, signed 'Cott Bridge', cross the stone bridge over the River Yeo and soon begin to climb an old green lane alongside Cott Down Plantation.

Continue past a barn, then at the woodland edge turn right on to a track and almost immediately climb a stile into the wood (NT sign). Proceed on a defined path through the wood, cross a stile, then keep to the left along the top edge of a field, following the line of trees to an arrowed stile.

Turn right along the field edge and soon descend into South Woolley Wood. At a junction of paths keep right through a gate and join a wide woodland track. Continue on this track through this delightful river valley, passing Tucker's Bridge, then in a quarter of a mile (0.4km) take the path waymarked '**Arlington Court** via Wilderness' right across the river to a gate and enter Smallacombe Meadow.

Ascend on a grassy path and soon enter the wooded area known as The Wilderness. At a fork keep left and gently ascend a gravel path, soon to pass a lily pond on the right. Bear right towards the church, go through the churchyard and soon rejoin your outward route back to the car park.

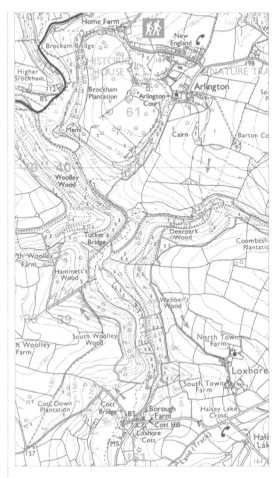

POINTS OF INTEREST

Arlington Court
Hidden among tree-lined lanes beside the hamlet of Arlington, is Arlington Court (1822) one of the few great houses of north Devon. The Chichester family owned the estate from 1384 until 1949, when Miss Rosalie Chichester died and left it to the National Trust. The plainness of the exterior belies its rich interior, for Miss Chichester was an avid collector of various *objets d'art*. Her acquisitions over the years included fascinating Victorian collections of model ships, seashells, pewter and snuff boxes. All her possessions were lovingly arranged with the fine furniture she had inherited, and the Trust has sensitively preserved the individuality of her home.

Arlington Park
A landscaped park surrounds Arlington Court and features a nature trail leading visitors down to the lake with its hide and waterfowl. Shetland ponies and Jacob sheep graze throughout the park. The obelisk seen in the park is a conical pile of white quartz which commemorates the jubilee of Queen Victoria on June 21 1887. The handsome stables contain one of the country's finest collections of carriages and horse-drawn vehicles; rides are available.

Barnstaple's covered Pannier Market is a highlight of any visit to the town

PANNIER MARKETS

There are a number of pannier markets in Devon, and the name has become associated with the buildings in which they are held. The name predates the buildings considerably, though, because originally the market traders would carry their goods for sale into the town in baskets or panniers and do their selling in the open air. In Barnstaple the market used to line the side of the High Street between Cross Street and lower Boutport Street, causing a considerable amount of congestion. This was eased by the construction of the present market building in 1855. Other pannier markets can still be found in Bideford, Dartmouth, Tavistock and Totnes.

BARNSTAPLE Map ref SS5633

Pay a flying visit to Barnstaple and you may be forgiven for thinking that it is a town much like any other. Its main shopping streets, partly pedestrianised, have the kind of stores you will see in any high street along with a modern shopping mall, but spend some time exploring the town and you will be well rewarded, for there are attractive little alleyways, quiet corners and some fine buildings. These include the covered Pannier Market, built in the mid-19th century, where traditional markets as well as craft and antiques markets are held. Part of the same development is Butcher's Row, built to house 33 butchers' shops, though it has now been infiltrated by greengrocers, fishmongers and delicatessens.

One of the most historic sites in Barnstaple is the huge mound created by the Normans as a vantage point for their castle, of which only fragments of the original wall remain. But Barnstaple's history goes back even further; records show that it was already the commercial centre for north Devon when it was granted a charter in AD 930 by King Æthelstan, grandson of Alfred the Great. It continued to prosper, becoming a major port for trade with America, and the ornate Queen Anne's Building down by the river dates from that era. Extensively renovated, this historic building is now open to the public and contains the excellent Barnstaple Heritage Centre, portraying the history of the town with interactive displays and 'face-to-face' speaking models of key figures from the town's past. These include the Elizabethan Town Clerk, Adam Wyatt, whose book *Lost Chronicle* is on sale in the Heritage Centre shop, and mistress Grace Beaple, who, during the Civil War, sheltered the prince (later Charles II). There are also reconstructions of the interior of a merchant's ship, a Civil War trench and scenes from medieval and Tudor Barnstaple. Upstream is the Long Bridge which is thought to have been originated in the 13th century.

Near the bridge is the Museum of North Devon which has a lively and imaginative range of exhibits, including a room which takes visitors into an underwater world, complete with sound effects, with giant turtles and large fish mounted on a realistic marine background. The display of North Devon pottery is quite spectacular and, of course, Tarka the Otter is never very far away (the Tarka Trail passes through the town – see page 44).

A little way north of the town are the internationally famous Marwood Hill Gardens which occupy about 12 acres of a sheltered valley. Delightful pathways lead down between the hillside trees and shrubs to a series of ponds, inhabited by some enormous koi carp.

BIDEFORD   Map ref SS4526

Bideford is a lovely little town with enormous character. Its focal point is the quay which was built in the 17th century and was a hive of activity in the town's seafaring heyday, when Bideford men were renowned for their seamanship. Those days are long gone now, but there are always a few coasters tied up alongside to keep alive something of the town's tradition, and they share the waters here with pleasure craft, including the boat for Lundy. The Torridge is spanned here by an ancient 24-arch stone bridge, but increasing traffic in the last few decades was seriously weakening it, and a new bridge and bypass now crosses high over the estuary further downstream – the views from it are wonderful.

BARNSTAPLE FAIR
This event has its origins far back in history, and is probably as old as the town itself. Beginning on the Wednesday before the 20th September, the festivities once followed on from the great annual market, but since markets have become more frequent occurrences the fair is now purely for ceremony and entertainment. The fair begins with the Town Council gathering in the Guildhall to make various toasts with a traditional spiced ale, then at midday a civic procession is formed and a proclamation read, a ceremony which is repeated at the southern end of the High Street and on the Strand. On the Saturday of that week a carnival, complete with decorated floats, takes place to raise money for local charities.

The curious overhang on the sturdy arches of the old bridge at Bideford is the result of road-widening over the years

*Clovelly owes its
preservation to Christine
Hamlyn, whose initials CH
adorn many of the cottages*

From the quay, a network of narrow streets and
alleyways (called 'drangs') climbs the hillside, lined with
good traditional butchers, bakers and greengrocers
alongside craft shops, art galleries, antiques and junk
shops – the traffic-free parts are particularly pleasant. A
steep climb leads to the Pannier Market, built in 1884,
though the market has been held since 1272. The Burton
Museum and Art Gallery hosts a wide variety of events,
and has a permanent gallery featuring the work of local
craftspeople.

Just west of Bideford, near Abbotsham, is The Big
Sheep, part of a large working sheep farm which has
been described by its owners as 'original, amusing and
bizarre'! It is also extremely interesting and informative,
with sheep milking, shearing, feeding of lambs,
sheepdog trials and spinning demonstrations, but the
abiding memory which most visitors take home with
them is of the hilarious sheep racing – and you can even
have whistle-blowing lessons.

CLOVELLY   Map ref SS3124

Of all Devon's pretty villages, this must surely be the
most famous and the most visited – which can make it
too crowded for comfort at the height of the season. You
need stamina to visit Clovelly. Its single cobbled street
has an alarming gradient which drops some 400 feet
(122m) in less than half a mile (0.8km), and traffic is
banned, so visitors have to park at the top of the hill and
explore on foot. Two things you should be aware of:
because of the steep cobbles, wear sensible footwear;
secondly, visitors enter the village through the visitor
centre and pay an admission fee. But if all this strikes
you as too commercialised, don't be put off, because
Clovelly is well worth it. If the narrow cobbled street

wasn't picturesque enough, the delightful little colour-washed 16th-century cottages that cluster along its slopes are decked with colourful flowers and shrubs, and at the bottom is the lovely little harbour.

If you find walking back up the street a trial, spare a thought for those who live here – everything, from food to fuel and furniture, has to be carried down this street, or lowered on sleds. A word of comfort for those who may be weak of leg and short of breath – there is a Land Rover service (Easter–Oct) to the car park by a back route.

On the way to Clovelly along the A39 near Bucks Mills is the Hobby Drive. It was constructed as a hobby (hence the name) by the local landowner in the 19th century, Sir James Hamlyn Williams. It is closed to traffic now, but offers a lovely 3-mile (4.8km) walk through wooded slopes above the coastline.

COMBE MARTIN Map ref SS5846

Combe Martin is said to be the largest village in Devon, and, as it is strung out along a narrow valley, its other claim to fame is to have the longest main street (about 2 miles/3.2km) of any village in the country. The 17th-century Pack O' Cards pub stands out amongst the otherwise standard seaside village architecture. Its construction was financed from the winnings from a card game, so it was built with four storeys to represent the four suits in a pack; each floor has 13 doors, for the cards in each suit, and there are 52 windows, the number of cards in the pack. No special architectural features represent the jokers in a pack, but no doubt there are those among the clientele who compensate for this oversight.

Though Combe Martin may not be one of the prettiest places, it does meet the sea at a nice little rocky bay with a sandy beach and lots of rock pools at low tide. In the centre of the village is the Combe Martin Motorcycle Collection, and even if you are not an enthusiast, this museum is fun to visit. Each visitor is

BUCKS MILLS

A little way along the coast from Clovelly is its delightful little neighbour, Bucks Mills, also perched on ground which rises steeply from a little beach and harbour. A winding lane descends through a beautiful wooded valley to the village, which, like Clovelly, has no room for visitors' cars and a car park has been provided a little way up the valley.

Wonderful old machines and motorcycling paraphernalia can be seen at the splendid Combe Martin Motorcycle Collection

HUNTING THE EARL

If you are in Combe Martin over the Spring Bank Holiday, you will witness the Hunting of the Earl of Rone, a ceremony with its roots in pagan times, but which has adapted over the centuries to incorporate other historical events. The original Hobby Horse procession is now preceded by a chase through the woods in pursuit of the 'Earl', who is then placed backwards on a donkey and led in the main procession to the beach, where he is unceremoniously dumped in the sea. The entire ceremony was banned in the mid-19th century due to excessive drunkenness and general bad behaviour, but enjoys a far better reputation these days.

BRIGHT AND BEAUTIFUL
Dunster and its surroundings are believed by some to have been the inspiration for the hymn *All Things Bright and Beautiful*, written by Mrs C Alexander. The Luttrells represented 'the rich man in his castle', Dunkery Beacon was 'the purple-headed mountain' and the Avill was 'the river running by'. The view from the top of Grabbist Hill, behind Dunster, certainly endorses the theory. In medieval times the slopes of the hill were terraced for viticulture, while the Giant's Chair, a natural amphitheatre on the side of the hill, was the legendary seat of a Cornish giant whose benevolence included helping Dunster housewives with their laundry – if they waved to him, he would wave back, causing a wind to dry their washing.

Dunster's broad main street is dominated by the castle, set high on its wooded hill

handed a 20-question quiz sheet at the entrance and all the answers can be found around the museum, injecting a bit of excitement into discovering things that you previously never needed to know.

The Wildlife Park near by is set in woodland with streams, cascading waterfalls and beautiful ornamental gardens. Its inhabitants include otters and the delightful meerkats, which have as their home the largest enclosure (a man-made desert) in Europe. On the road to Ilfracombe, Watermouth Castle is great fun for children, with attractions ranging from adventure playgrounds to fairy-tale tableaux to antique penny-in-the-slot machines and 'dancing water' shows.

DUNSTER Somerset Map ref SS9943

On the eastern edge of Exmoor, Dunster is one of the most picturesque medieval villages in the country, complete with a huge Norman castle which dominates the entire area. Now in the care of the National Trust, Dunster Castle was substantially altered in the early 17th century and further work was carried out in 1868, but its medieval character was preserved to a large extent. The oak-panelled halls have magnificent ceilings and there are many reminders of the Luttrell family who called this home for some 600 years until 1950.

The village is one of the loveliest in Britain, its medieval character perfectly preserved. The main street of pretty little shops and tearooms sits cosily between two high wooded hills, one topped by the castle, and is distinguished by the octagonal Yarn Market, a relic of its days as an important wool centre.

EXMOOR Devon/Somerset

Exmoor has some wonderful and varied scenery. On the coast between Combe Martin and Countisbury, rivers which rise on the open moorland have cut deep ravines, meeting the sea between enormous rock faces which rise almost vertically from the water, forming some of the highest cliffs in Britain. Inland is the high moorland plateau, with deep wooded valleys and charming little villages such as Winsford, Selworthy and Allerford.

The 267-square-mile National Park was established in 1954 to preserve a unique and beautiful landscape, but most of it remains in private ownership and continues to be farmed. However, visitors enjoy considerable freedom to explore the countryside, and the best way to do this is on foot or on horseback. Some of the best woodland walks are around Dulverton, Dunster and Cloutsham, and on the coast path. About 12,000 acres of the moor are owned and conserved by the National Trust, including Watersmeet, the park's most famous beauty spot (see page 33).

Britain's largest wild animal, the red deer, survives on Exmoor, but easier to see are the sturdy little Exmoor ponies that roam the moor, believed to be directly descended from the prehistoric wild horse. Overhead, the sight of the buzzard is not uncommon, and there are fulmars and oystercatchers along the coast. One way to be sure of seeing a large variety of birds and animals is to visit the delightful Exmoor Zoological Park at South Stowford, 12 acres of landscaped gardens and informal paddocks amidst lovely rural countryside. To get a good introduction to Exmoor as a whole, visit one of the excellent museums – the Lyn and Exmoor at Lynton and the West Somerset Rural Life Museum at Allerford are particularly recommended.

The landscape near Malmsmead was evoked to great effect by R D Blackmore in his romantic novel Lorna Doone *(1869); the author spent much of his childhood around Exmoor*

LORNA DOONE
The deep combes and heather-clad moorland around Malmsmead and Oare were the setting of R D Blackmore's famous story of the tragic heroine, Lorna Doone and her lawless family. The story is said to be based on the reality of a family of Scottish outlaws who came to Exmoor, failed to support themselves from farming and turned instead to a life of crime. 'Doone Valley', as it is now known, is the focus of many special walking, horse-riding and motor tours.

Ancient folds and twists in the rock mark the dramatic cliffs at Hartland Point

THE LOST QUAY

Visitors to Hartland Quay may wonder where the quay is, and the answer is that it has gone. It was originally constructed in the 16th century at the instigation of no less a group of seafarers than Sir Francis Drake, Sir Walter Raleigh and Sir John Hawkins. Hartland Quay was the only harbour on this dangerous stretch of coastline, and, even so, it was not an easy one to navigate. None but the best seamen could successfully negotiate their vessels into and out of the harbour and the stormy seas finally destroyed the fabric of the quay in the 19th century.

HARTLAND   Map ref SS2524

To many people, Hartland Point is more dramatic than Land's End. It looks out over one of the most treacherous stretches of water in Britain, with dangerous currents and huge jagged rocks. Even on the calmest of days, the waters swirl menacingly around the headland, and in a storm the crashing waves are spectacular. Just to the east is lovely, unspoilt Shipload Bay (National Trust) practically inaccessible since the steps leading to the beach were damaged. Hartland Quay is 3 miles (4.8km) in the other direction (see Walk on page 24), but you don't have to walk – there is good access by road and plenty of parking, especially at the lowest level, where there is a hotel, a shop and museum, above the rocky beach. The little museum is all about seafaring.

The village of Hartland, some way inland, is pleasant but unremarkable, but its parish church at nearby Stoke is a real treasure, its size out of all proportion to the community it serves. Also near by is Hartland Abbey, an 18th-century Gothic-style mansion which was built on the site of a 12th-century Augustinian monastery.

ILFRACOMBE   Map ref SS5247

The largest resort on the north Devon coast, Ilfracombe is largely a Victorian creation, and the fact that it has remained popular when so many of Britain's seaside resorts have gone into a decline is largely due to its setting on one of the most beautiful stretches of coastline in the country. The town is more attractive than many, with some beautiful gardens and a busy little harbour, crammed with pleasure craft and fishing boats.

Ilfracombe is set in a cradle of hills, all with wonderful views – Hillsborough Hill is now a nature reserve with paths leading up to its 447-foot (136-m) summit; Lantern Hill, above the harbour, is surmounted by an ancient chapel which served as a lighthouse for over five centuries and is appropriately dedicated to the patron saint of sailors, St Nicholas; the Torrs Walks rise to 640 feet (136m) in gentle fashion, with lots of seats on the way. Walkers can also zigzag their way up to the 156-foot (48m) summit of Capstone Hill.

Of course, you can't have a seaside resort without a beach, and Ilfracombe has several – the unique Tunnels Beaches are approached from the bottom of Northfield Road through tunnels cut through the cliffs and surrounded by towering rock faces; others are Wildermouth Beach, Cheyne Beach, Larkstone Beach, Rapparee Cove and Hele Bay.

Ilfracombe's attractions include its superb arts complex – the Landmark – in a distinctive modern building on the seafront, a splendid town museum and the superbly restored 16th-century corn mill and pottery at Hele Bay, with an overshot waterwheel powering the machinery to produce wholemeal flour. Chambercombe Manor, in a pretty, sheltered combe on the edge of the town, is one of the oldest manor houses in England, of Norman origins. Subsequently enlarged, it now has a rambling appearance, an uneven roofline and a cobbled courtyard.

ILFRACOMBE FESTIVALS
Ilfracombe is very active in promoting itself to visitors, and as well as the traditional entertainments and attractions, it now stages a number of festivals during the summer, including the Victorian Week in June when the whole town steps back in time for costumed events and street markets. During the week-long National Youth Arts Festival around 1,000 performers invade the town to stage all kinds of music, theatre and exhibitions, both undercover and out in the streets.

The largely Victorian resort of Ilfracombe spreads inland from the sheltered harbour with its tiny chapel

Dramatic Cliffs and Waterfalls Near Hartland Quay

An exciting and bracing cliff walk along part of north Devon's most exposed and remote coast, returning along quiet inland tracks. Although fairly short, the walk features a quay and small museum, a waterfall, an ancient mill and a splendid church. A couple of ups and downs, otherwise easy going underfoot.

Time: 2½–3 hours. Distance: 4 miles (6.4km).
Location: 17 miles (27.4km) west of Bideford.
Start: Car park above Hartland Quay. (OS grid ref: SS223247.)
OS Map: Explorer 126 (Clovelly & Hartland)
1:25,000.
See Key to Walks on page 121.

ROUTE DIRECTIONS

Take the waymarked stony path at the southern end of the car park above **Hartland Quay** and head uphill, soon to turn right at a fingerpost on to the well-established coast path. Round a headland and begin to descend gently to follow a grassy path inland around **St Catherine's Tor**.

Cross stepping stones over a stream, bear diagonally left with marker to a wooden gate and turn right and steadily climb uphill on the cliff path to a ladder stile.

Shortly, descend steeply on a stony path to a grassy plateau by **Speke's Mill Mouth Waterfall**.

Turn left along a wide track and head inland, ignoring the coast path arrowed right. Stay on this track through the valley, parallel to the stream, to a metalled lane. Turn left to reach a crossroads at Lymebridge.

Turn right to visit **Docton Mill**, otherwise follow the lane left and steadily ascend, passing the entrance to Trellick House to reach a further crossroads (Kernstone Cross). Proceed straight ahead on to a track signed 'unsuitable for motors', then, on arriving at Wargery Farm, bear left on to an unmetalled green lane.

Keep to this rough track passing through a deep valley, then, in the hamlet of Stoke, keep ahead at a crossroads to reach the main street. Turn left and enter **St Nectan's** churchyard.

Leave the churchyard via a

Docton Mill at Hartland offers a welcome opportunity for a break

stile in the far corner and follow the waymarked path in front of houses and across driveways, parallel to the lane, to a stile and open field. Keep left-handed along the hedge, climb a stone wall stile and proceed to a stile behind a small building. Turn right on to the coast path and shortly bear right along the metalled lane down to Hartland Quay and the car park.

POINTS OF INTEREST

Hartland Quay
Hartland Quay was once a thriving port, where for over 250 years boats brought in supplies of coal, lime, slate, grain and building supplies to this remote part of Devon. After constant battering by storms, the harbour began to break up in 1893 and by the 1920s it had all gone. All that remains are the former harbour buildings, now comprising a hotel, shop and small museum illustrating the history of this fascinating place.

St Catherine's Tor
Although much of this prominent mass of rock and cliff has fallen into the sea, it is said to have been surmounted by a Roman villa, or a chapel dedicated to the saint.

Speke's Mill Mouth Waterfall
This is one of the finest waterfalls on the north Devon coast. A stream tumbles 150 feet (46m) in a series of waterfalls to the beach, gradually cut back inland along a fault in the folded strata.

Docton Mill
A fully restored watermill built on a site first worked by the Saxons. No corn has been ground here since 1914 and the waterwheel now generates electricity to heat the house. There are delightful grounds to stroll around in the summer, including orchards, wild woodland and the colourful flower-filled waterfall and mill gardens.

St Nectan's Church, Stoke
The magnificent tower of Hartland's 14th-century church rises to 128 feet (39m), making it the second highest tower in Devon. Dedicated to the 5th-century Celtic saint, Nectan, its fine interior is noted for the delicate 15th-century rood-screen, the well-preserved wagon roof and the carved font which dates from Norman times. An informal small church museum is housed in the Pope's Chamber above the north porch, and displays, among other items, the village stocks and medieval tiles.

Tapeley Park is famous for its formal Italianate gardens, laid out earlier this century

MUSICAL CEILINGS

A musical connection rather more obscure than the Christie's operatic ones exists in some of the decorative ceilings at Tapeley. They were crafted in the 18th century by a group of travelling Italian musicians who, when musical engagements were sparse, would turn their hand to plasterwork instead – a novel variation on the more usual notion of musicians getting 'plastered'!

INSTOW Map ref SS4730

More low-key than most of its neighbours, Instow is a charming little place at the wide estuary of the rivers Taw and Torridge with a sandy beach backed by low dunes. Standing high on a hill overlooking the estuary is Tapeley Park, the home of the Christie family who are famous for their operatic connections (notably at Glyndebourne), and a collection of operatic costumes is on display in the house. The house (tours by arrangement only) also contains some fine pieces of furniture and an interesting collection of porcelain, but the gardens are the real attraction. Rare and tender shrubs, including palms, mimosa and hibiscus, thrive amongst the beautiful terraces of these sheltered slopes, and there is a new organic permaculture garden. And, everywhere you go, there are wonderful views over the Torridge estuary and the north Devon coast.

LUNDY Map ref SS0345

The sight of a distant island has always stirred up our instincts for exploration and adventure, and there are few places along the north Devon coast which don't have sight of Lundy. The boat trip is expensive, but it is money well spent, for Lundy has an enormous variety of things to see and do. It is reached by boat, the MS *Oldenburg*, from either Bideford or Ilfracombe and after a 2-hour trip, passengers are transferred by smaller boat to the beach landing point. Obviously, a clear day is essential if you are not to miss the breathtaking scenery around Lundy's coastline, and do try to avoid excessively windy days because although Lundy has a generally equable climate, the Atlantic winds sweep uninterrupted across the island from the west.

Just over 3 miles (4.8km) long and about half a mile (0.8km) across at its widest point, Lundy has granite cliffs rising to over 400 feet (122m) and the land varies from rough grazing in the north to fertile farm land in the south. It is best known for its breeding colony of puffins, but visitors will see many other kinds of birds, as well as seals, basking sharks, sika deer, mountain goats and Lundy ponies. But wildlife is not the only attraction, there is a great deal of evidence of the island's fascinating history, including an ancient burial chamber and a cave which was used for a while as a prison; you can also see the cannon which were fired in Georgian times as a fog warning and a chasm which opened up when tremors from the Lisbon earthquake in 1755 reached Lundy. The hub of Lundy's social life is the Marisco Tavern, a friendly pub with its own Lundy beer.

All of Lundy is beautiful, but the most spectacular views can be enjoyed from the west side. If wild plants are your particular interest, explore the eastern side, and if you are a climber there are over 60 challenging rock faces which can be tackled, though 38 of these are closed during the seabird breeding season (April to July).

PUFFIN ISLAND
The name 'Lundy' is derived from the Norse words 'Lund', puffin, and 'ey', island, so we know that the Viking raiders of the 9th century were familiar with this great rock in the Bristol Channel. Less surprising, perhaps, is the knowledge that the island was a haunt of smugglers in the 18th century – Benson's Cove, in the southeast, was where they stored their contraband.

Sticking up from the rocks below the cliff, the aptly-named Needle Rock is a clear landmark on Lundy's western shore

A REMARKABLE RESCUE
In 1899, on a stormy night in January, a ship in difficulty was sighted some way along the coast, but because of the high seas and weather conditions, the Lynmouth lifeboat could not be launched. Rather than leave the stricken crew to their fate, a decision was taken to try to haul the lifeboat along the coast to another launching place, a distance of 13 miles (20.8km) which included Countisbury and Porlock Hills. A dozen horses and up to a hundred helpers struggled against tremendous odds, widening the road as they went, removing gates and walls, repairing broken wheels on the enormous carriage. At 6 o'clock the following morning the lifeboat was successfully launched and the vessel and its crew were saved.

HOW TO OFFEND A HERRING
Lynmouth was once noted for the particularly large catches of herrings that its fishermen would bring home. Then in 1823 the herrings deserted the area, a phenomenon which has a choice of local explanations. Some say that it was because the local church was extracting a herring tithe from the locals, a particularly unpopular tax. The herring, apparently, couldn't bear to be the cause of such contention. Another version is that, because there were more herring than the fishermen could eat or sell, they were used as manure on the land – insulted, the herring departed, never to return.

The spectacular Valley of the Rocks, west of Lynton, opposite

LYNTON AND LYNMOUTH   Map ref SS7249

These twin villages are set amidst some of the best scenery on the north coast. Lynton is perched on top of the 500-foot (152m) cliff, while Lynmouth nestles at its foot, where the lovely East Lyn River flows down to meet the sea at the charming little harbour. Pretty cottages line the road beside the river, with a cluster of gift and tea shops, bed and breakfast places and a thatched pub, but although the village has inevitably become somewhat touristy, this does not detract from its undeniable charm.

Lynton is not nearly as picturesque as it neighbour, but it is nevertheless a pleasant little town, and it does have magnificent views along the coast. Among its most interesting buildings is the impressive Town Hall, just one of the benefits endowed by Sir George Newnes, publisher of the Sherlock Holmes stories, among other things, who was a frequent visitor in the 19th century. He also put most of the money into the cliff railway, which links the two communities. Opened at Easter 1890, the railway descends the 500-foot (152m) cliff at a gradient of 1-in-1¾ and its two cars (one going up and one going down) are linked by steel cable. The descending car is propelled by the weight of 700 gallons of water, pumped into its tank at the top of the cliff and emptied at the bottom, and this action hauls the ascending car up to the top.

One of the oldest cottages in Lynton, a delightful 18th-century whitewashed cottage opposite the school, is now the home of the fascinating Lyn and Exmoor Museum, with a collection of bygones which illustrates the life and work of the population. Among its collections are traditional arts and crafts, a scale model of the old Lynton to Barnstaple railway, a reconstruction of an Exmoor kitchen of the 1800s and a section devoted to the tragic Lynmouth flood of 15th August 1952 which claimed 34 lives and devastated the harbour village. It has been estimated that some 90 million gallons of rain fell in one night on the 40 square miles around Lynmouth. Tiny streams became raging torrents, which combined to pour down the valley, sweeping away the buildings of Lynmouth in their path. The level that the waters attained is marked on a wall at the foot of the Glen Lyn Gorge.

The remarkable Valley of the Rocks, one mile (1.6km) outside Lynton, is unlike the many combes which run down to the sea along this stretch of coast in that it runs parallel to the coast, a dry valley which was probably formed during the Ice Ages. The great jagged rocks which protrude skywards from the grassy valley create strange formations which have been endowed with such fanciful names as The Devil's Cheesewring, Ragged Jack and Castle Rocks. A remarkable sight on their own, these rocks are often joined in picturesque pose by one of the wild goats which inhabit the area.

Exmoor and the North Coast's Wooded Combes

This 50-mile (80-km) tour takes in the beautiful wooded combes of the north Devon coast, the rolling pastures of its hinterland and the wild open moorland of western Exmoor, before visiting the beauty spot of Watersmeet. The early part of the drive is on steep, narrow roads with hairpin bends – it is slow going, but the scenery is well worth the time it takes.

ROUTE DIRECTIONS

See Key to Car Tours on page 120.

From the town hall and tourist information office in Lynton, follow signs for the Valley of the Rocks, which is reached shortly after leaving the town. This beautiful valley has huge, grotesque rock formations jutting out of its grassy slopes, populated by wild goats. From the road there are tantalising glimpses of the sea and a walk here will be even more rewarding. There is a picnic area on the left at the start of the valley and a large parking area, the last until the end of the valley, on the right.

The road passes into the Lee Valley Estate and continues past Lee Abbey Christian Community. Just under 2 miles (3.2km) from Lynton, the toll point is reached. Follow the narrow, winding road, which turns away from the coast, through steep, wooded combes, for three quarters of a mile (1.2km). At the next fork take the right (lower) road, signposted 'Woody Bay'. Pass the Woody Bay Hotel and a National Trust car park on the left, then in one mile (1.6km) at a T-junction turn right. In another mile (1.6km), just past a telephone box, take the right fork downhill, signed 'Hunter's Inn, Heddons Mouth, Trentishoe'.

In 3 miles (4.8km) meet the A39 and turn right, signposted 'Barnstaple'. After 3½ miles (5.6km) turn left on to the A399, signposted 'South Molton'. Detour to visit Arlington Court, turn right, then left, signed 'Barnstaple', and continue for 3¼ miles (5.2km) before turning left, signposted **'Arlington Court'**. This charming house (NT) dates from 1822 and contains some fascinating collections.

On the main route, continue with hilly agricultural land on both sides of the road. In another 2¼ miles (3.6km) detour right to visit the lovely **Exmoor Zoological Park**, where a wide variety of birds and animals can be viewed within an attractive landscaped garden setting.

Return to the A399 and turn right. In 12¾ miles (20.5km) at a roundabout, take the 2nd exit, signposted 'South Molton' and continue for 1½ miles (2.4km) into the town. South Molton, with some elegant Georgian

Lynmouth huddles round the harbour at the cliff foot

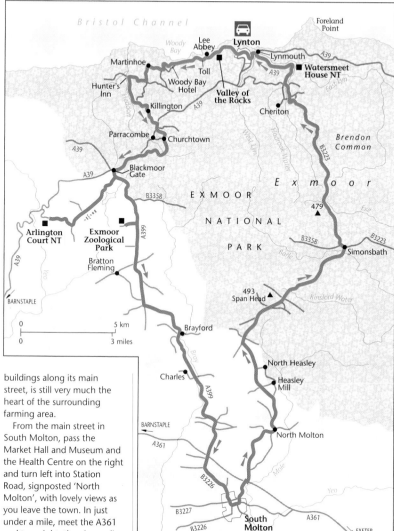

buildings along its main street, is still very much the heart of the surrounding farming area.

From the main street in South Molton, pass the Market Hall and Museum and the Health Centre on the right and turn left into Station Road, signposted 'North Molton', with lovely views as you leave the town. In just under a mile, meet the A361 and turn right, then immediately left, still signposted 'North Molton', and continue for 2¼ miles (3.6km) into the village. Just past a petrol station on the left, turn left, signposted 'Heasley Mill' and 'Simonsbath'. In 1½ miles (2.4km) bear left, signposted 'North Heasley' and 'Simonsbath'. In half a mile (0.8km) at crossroads keep forward, signposted 'Simonsbath' and in 1¾ miles

(2.8km) at a T-junction turn right again, signposted 'Simonsbath' and 'Exford' to climb steadily on to Exmoor. In 5¼ miles (8.4km) turn left on to the B3223, signposted 'Lynton'. In 6 miles (9.7km) turn right on to the A39, signposted 'Lynmouth and Watersmeet'. Watersmeet is one of the county's premier beauty spots, and the waters

that meet here, the East Lyn River and Hoaroak Water, do so in a deep, wooded valley with footpaths leading off in either direction.

Continue down the wooded valley to return to Lynmouth, prettily set around the river valley and tiny harbour, and Lynton, looking out from the clifftop. The two are linked by a cliff railway.

ANCHORING THE SHIFTING SANDS

The partnership between the shifting sands and marram grass is a remarkable one. Little will grow in the dry, constantly moving environment of the fine sand, but marram grass thrives on it, being stimulated into vigorous growth (up to one metre a year) the more the sands are blown around. In return, the marram traps the sand between its stems and this eventually leads to the land becoming stabilised. When this happens, the marram dies back to allow other plants to flourish, but any reversal of this and it springs back into life and the process starts all over again.

Coarse marram grass holds in check the dunes behind the magnificent expanse of Saunton Sands

SAUNTON SANDS AND BRAUNTON BURROWS
Map ref SS4535

Saunton Sands is one of the best beaches in Devon, a 3-mile (4.8km) curve of golden sands backed by grassy dunes which has remained surprisingly unspoilt. Towards the northern end of the beach is a car park with a small shop, toilets and a café, and it is at this end that most visitors tend to congregate, particularly those with young families who arrive with all the necessary paraphernalia. The surfers, too, make a bee-line from the car park to the sea, but if you are prepared to walk a little way southwards the rewards are well worth the effort. You will probably be able to find your own little enclave amongst the dunes, with an uninterrupted walk across the sands to the sea, where you can swim without having to watch out for surfboards. Be warned, though, that the very southern end of the beach has treacherous currents which make swimming dangerous.

It is better to turn inland here and explore the wonderful Braunton Burrows. This incorporates one of the largest sand dune systems in Britain and is internationally famous for its plant and animal life. Marram grass holds the sands in place here, and where the ground has stabilised, other plants, such as stonecrop, viper's bugloss and evening primrose, carpet the ground with splashes of colour. In the damper areas there are the marsh varieties of marigolds, orchids and helleborines. Large flocks of wading birds populate the adjacent estuary, and migrating birds rest here. This is also an entymologist's paradise, with an enormous variety of moths and butterflies. The Ministry of Defence leases a small area of the reserve for training purposes, so watch out for the red warning flags which are flown when exercises are in progress.

WATERSMEET Map ref SS7448

This renowned beauty spot, now in the care of the
National Trust, can be reached on footpaths along the
leafy valley from Lynmouth or by car. Once at
Watersmeet, the network of riverside paths expands to
give walkers plenty of choice. The waters that meet here
are the East Lyn River and Hoaroak Water, both of which
take the form of a series of pools, with water tumbling
from one to another over the rocks. Lucky visitors may
even see salmon leaping amidst the falls and rapids. The
steep sides of the valley are heavily wooded, mostly
sessile oak, with some beech and larch, with an
undergrowth of ferns, mosses and an abundance of wild
flowers. The National Trust have an information centre,
shop and tea rooms at Watersmeet House, a former
fishing lodge which dates from the early 19th century.

WOOLACOMBE AND MORTEHOE Map ref SS4643

The lovely sandy beach of Woolacombe and the
delightful rocky cove at Mortehoe have made these twin
villages a magnet for holiday-makers in the summer, but
the surrounding area is still unmistakably agricultural.
Mortehoe sits high on the cliffs above the rocky
coastline between Morte Point and Woolacombe sands
and has wonderful views. Its 12th-century church is said
to contain the tomb of one of the murderers of Thomas
à Becket. Woolacombe is very much a family resort, with
children's entertainment and play areas, and evening
entertainment is mainly of the disco or live pub music
variety, though there is a repertory theatre giving two
performances a week in the summer season.

*The scenic valley of
Watersmeet, east of
Lynmouth, features leafy
walks*

INDUSTRY IN THE VALLEY
It is hard to believe, when
walking through the peaceful,
leafy valley at Watersmeet,
that it was once a hive of
activity with an iron mine,
charcoal burners, lime kilns
and a hydro-electric power
plant. The power station, one
of the first of its kind in
Britain, supplied Lynton and
Lynmouth from 1890 until it
was swept away in the great
flood of 1952. It was also the
last supply of 110 cycles per
second electricity in the
country.

Exmoor and the North Coast

Leisure Information

Places of Interest

Shopping

The Performing Arts

Sports, Activities and the Outdoors

Annual Events and Customs

Checklist

Leisure Information

TOURIST INFORMATION CENTRES

Barnstaple
36 Boutport Street. Tel: 01271 375000.
Bideford
The Quay. Tel: 01237 477676.
Combe Martin
SeaCot, Cross Street (seasonal). Tel: 01271 883319.
Ilfracombe
Landmark Theatre, Sea Front. Tel: 0845 458 3630.
Lynton
Town Hall. Tel: 01598 752225.

EXMOOR NATIONAL PARK VISITOR CENTRES

Exmoor National Park Authority
Exmoor House, Dulverton, Somerset. Tel: 01398 323665.
Combe Martin
Seacot, Cross Street. Tel: 01271 883319 (seasonal).
County Gate
Where the A39 crosses Devon/Somerset boundary. Tel: 01598 741321 (seasonal).
Dulverton
7–9 Fore Street. Tel: 01398 323841. Limited winter opening.
Dunster
Dunster Steep. Tel: 01643 821835.

Lynmouth
The Esplanade. Tel: 01598 752509 (limited winter opening).

OTHER INFORMATION

Devon Wildlife Trust
Shirehampton House, 35–37 St David's Hill, Exeter. Tel: 01392 279244.
English Heritage
29 Queen Square, Bristol. Tel: 0117 975 0700. www.english-heritage.org.uk
Forest Enterprise England
340 Bristol Business Park, Coldharbour Lane, Bristol. Tel: 0117 906 6000.
National Trust for Devon
Killerton House, Broadclyst, Exeter. Tel: 01392 881691. www.nationaltrust.org.uk
English Nature Devonteam
Level 2 Renslade House, Bonhay Road, Exeter. Tel: 01392 88970.
Parking
Visitor's Permit, for long stay car parks in Barnstaple, Ilfracombe, Combe Martin, Croyde, Lynton and Lynmouth and Mortehoe from Tourist Information Centres or North Devon District Council. Tel: 01271 388279.
South West Lakes Trust
Highercombe Park, Lewdown, Okehampton. Tel: 01837 871565.

ORDNANCE SURVEY MAPS

Landranger 1:50,000. Sheets 180, 181. Outdoor Leisure 1:25,000 Sheet 9

Places of Interest

Unless otherwise stated, there will be an admission charge to the following places of interest.
Arlington Court
Arlington. Tel: 01271 850296. Open Apr–early Nov, most days.
Barnstaple Heritage Centre
Queen Anne's Walk, The Strand. Tel: 01271 373003. Open all year, most days.
Chambercombe Manor
Ilfracombe. Tel: 01271 862624. Open Easter–Sep, daily, except Sat.
The Combe Martin Motorcycle Collection
Cross Street, Combe Martin. Tel: 01271 882346. Open mid-May to end Oct, daily.
Combe Martin Wildlife Park
Combe Martin. Tel: 01271 882486. Open Mar–early Nov, daily.
Dunster Castle
Tel: 01643 821314. Open: garden and grounds daily; castle Apr–early Nov, most days.

Dunster Watermill
Dunster. Tel: 01643 821759.
Open Apr–Oct, most days.
Exmoor Zoological Park
South Stowford, Bratton
Fleming. Tel: 01598 763352.
Open early Feb to mid-Nov.
Hartland Abbey & Gardens
Hartland. Tel: 01237 441264.
Open Apr–Oct.
Hartland Quay Museum
Hartland. Tel: 01288 331353.
Open Easter & Whit–Sep,
daily.
Hele Mill
Hele Bay, Ilfracombe. Tel: 01271
863185. Open Easter Sun–Oct,
most days.
Ilfracombe Museum
Wilder Road. Tel: 01271
863541. Open Apr–Oct daily;
Nov–Mar closed weekends.
Lyn and Exmoor Museum
Market Street, Lynton.
Tel: 01598 752205. Open
Easter–Oct, daily, except Sat.
Marwood Hill Gardens
Barnstaple. Tel: 01271 342528.
Open all year, daily.
Museum of North Devon
The Square, Barnstaple. Tel:
01271 346747. Open all year,
Tue–Sat.
**North Devon Maritime
Museum**
Odun Road, Appledore.
Tel: 01237 474852. Open
Easter–Oct, daily.
Tapeley Park Gardens
Instow. Tel: 01271 342371/
860528. Open mid-Mar to Oct,
daily except Sat. House tours by
arrangement only.

SPECIAL INTEREST FOR CHILDREN

The following places may be of
interest to visitors with children.
Unless otherwise stated, there
will be an admission charge.
The Big Sheep
Abbotsham, near Bideford. Tel:
01237 4723656. Open all year
daily.
Exmoor Zoological Park
South Stowford, Bratton
Fleming. Tel: 01598 763352.
Open early Feb to mid-Nov.
**The Milky Way and North
Devon Bird of Prey Centre**
Clovelly. Tel: 01237 431255.
Open Apr–Oct, daily; Nov–Mar

most days.
Watermouth Castle
Ilfracombe. Tel: 01271 867474.
Open Apr–Oct, most days.

Shopping

Bideford
Art galleries and craft shops.
Pannier Market Tue and Sat.
Open-air market Wed mid-May
to mid-Sep.
Barnstaple
Pannier Market Tue, Fri and Sat.
Craft market Mon and Thu
Apr–Christmas.
Cattle market Sat.
Antiques market Wed.
Dunster
Market Mon and Fri.

LOCAL SPECIALITIES

Clotted Cream
Many local shops send cream by
post.
Dried Flowers
Rosehill, West Pristacott Farm,
Harracott, Newton Tracey,
Barnstaple.
Tel: 01271 858446.
**Fresh and Smoked Fish
Products**
Blakewell Fisheries, Muddiford,
near Barnstaple. Tel: 01271
344533.
Glass
Exmoor Glass, Porlock Weir.
Tel: 01643 863141.
Hand-Spun Woollens
The Big Sheep, Abbotsham, near
Bideford.
Paintings
The Millwheel Gallery, High
Street, Porlock. Tel: 01643
862238.
Pottery
Brannam's Pottery, Roundswell
Industrial Estate, Barnstaple.
Tel: 01271 343035.

The Performing Arts

College Theatre
Abbotsham Road, Bideford.
Contact Tourist Information
Office.
Queen's Theatre
Boutport Street, Barnstaple.
Tel: 01271 324242.
Landmark Theatre
Sea Front, Ilfracombe.
Tel: 01271 324242.

*Celebrate Devon's maritime
traditions at the museum in
Appledore*

Sports, Activities and the Outdoors

ANGLING

Sea
Appledore: Fishing trips arranged
by Quay Cabin, 15A The Quay.
Tel: 01237 477505. *Barnstaple:*
Fishing trips arranged by The
Kingfisher Rod and Tackle Shop,
22 Castle Street. Also fly tuition.
Tel: 01271 344919.
Lynton & Lynmouth: Fishing trips
from the harbour.
Fly
Blakewell Trout Farm and
Fishery, Muddiford, Barnstaple.
Tel: 01271 344533. Wimbleball
Lake. Tel: 01837 871565.
Coarse
Permits for Jennetts, Bideford;
Slade Reservoirs, Ilfracombe
contact South West Lakes Trust
Tel: 01837 871565.

BEACHES

Combe Martin
Pebbles and sand. Dogs allowed.
Croyde
Flat, sandy beach. Dogs
restricted. Lifeguards patrol end
May to mid-Sep.
Ilfracombe
Tunnels Beaches: shale with grey
sand, seawater swimming pool
(tidal). Wildermouth: pebble
beach. Hele Bay: shale.
Instow
Promenade and clean stretch of

sand. Dogs restricted. Lifeguards patrol mid-June to early Sep.
Putsborough
Sandy beach with rock pools. Dogs restricted. Easter–Oct.
Saunton Sands
Long sandy beach. Dogs allowed. Lifeguards patrol mid-June to early Sep.
Welcombe
Rocky beach, sand at low tide; approach down narrow bumpy lane; limited parking.
Westward Ho!
Sand, pebbles. Dogs restricted in certain areas May–Sep. Lifeguards patrol Jun–early Sep.
Woolacombe
Long flat sandy beach. EC Blue Flag. Dogs restricted to certain areas. Lifeguards patrol end May to mid-Sep.

BOAT TRIPS

Motor launches operate from Ilfracombe Pier and Harbour. Trips to Lundy from Bideford and Ilfracombe, coastal cruises to Woolacombe, Lynmouth and Exmoor.
Appledore
Tarka Cruises, Trips from The Quay. Tel: 01237 476191.
Ilfracombe
Paddle steamers *Balmoral* and *Waverley* sail from Ilfracombe Pier. Tel: 0141 243 2234.

COUNTRY PARKS, FORESTS AND NATURE RESERVES

The Cairn and Old Railway, Ilfracombe. Tel: 01392 79244.
Dunster Forest. Tel: 01398 323665.
Gallox Hill, near Dunster. Tel: 01398 323665.
Grabbist Hill, near Dunster. Tel: 01398 323665.
Watersmeet. Tel: 01398 323665.

CYCLING

Information on cycle routes from local Tourist Information Centres. Dedicated BikeBuses no longer operate, but it is hoped that buses on the route between Plymouth and Barnstaple via Yelverton, Tavistock, Okehampton, Hatherleigh, Torrington and Bideford, will be adapted to

carry up to four cycles. For further information contact DevonBus Line Tel: 01392 382800.
For details of cycle routes in Devon visit www.devon.gov.uk/tourism/ncn

CYCLE HIRE

Barnstaple
Biketrail, Fremington Quay. Tel: 01271 372586.
Tarka Trail Cycle Hire, Railway Station. Tel: 01271 324202.
Bideford
Bideford Cycle Hire, Torrington Street, East the Water. Tel: 01237 424123.
Tarka Cycle Hire, The Railway Station, 14 Barnstaple Street. Tel: 01271 324202.
Otter Cycle Hire, Station Road, Braunton. Tel: 01271 813339.

GOLF COURSES

Ilfracombe
Ilfracombe Golf Club, Hele Bay. Tel: 01271 862176.
Saunton
Saunton Golf Club, nr Braunton. Tel: 01271 812436.
Torrington
Torrington Golf Club, Weare Trees. Tel: 01805 622229.
Westward Ho!
Royal North Devon Golf Club. Tel: 01237 473817.

GOLF DRIVING RANGES

Barnstaple
Portmore Golf Park, Landkey Road. Tel: 01271 378378.
Ilfracombe
Ilfracombe & Woolacombe Golf Range, Woolacombe Road. Tel: 01271 866222.

HORSE-RIDING

Lynton
Brendon Manor Farm. Tel: 01598 741246.
Woolacombe
Woolacombe Riding Stables, Eastacott Farm. Tel: 01271 870260.

SAILING

Ilfracombe
Ilfracombe Yacht Club, The Quay. Tel: 01271 863969.

SHOOTING

Ilfracombe
North Devon Shooting Ground, Bickenbridge Farm, near Mullacott Cross. Tel: 01271 863959.

WATERSPORTS

Bideford
Skern Lodge Outdoor Centre, Appledore. Tel: 01237 475992. Canoeing, waterskiing, sailing.

Annual Events and Customs

Appledore
Regatta, end July/early August.
Barnstaple
North Devon Show, Huntshaw Farm, early August.
Ancient Chartered Fair, mid-September.
Carnival Procession, mid-September.
Bideford
Water Festival, August.
Carnival, early September.
Regatta, early September.
Combe Martin
Hunting of the Earl of Rone, Spring Bank Holiday Weekend.
Carnival Week, early August.
Dunster
Country Fair, July.
Dunster Show, August.
Ilfracombe
Victorian Week, mid-June.
National Youth Arts Festival early July.
Fishing Festival end July/early August.
Carnival, late August.
Lynton & Lynmouth
Parracombe Revels, May Bank Holiday weekend.
Lyn and Exmoor Festival, mid–late June.
Westward Ho!
Potwalloping Festival, end May.

The checklists give details of just some of the facilities within the area covered by this guide. Further information can be obtained from Tourist Information Centres.

Devon's Rural Heartland

Major tourist attractions are few and far between in this area, which, in a way, makes it all the more interesting to visit because here you will find the real heart and the real people of Devon. Its towns are generally unspoilt by modern development and remain centres for the surrounding agricultural areas, with 'proper' markets and practical shops, and if you delve beneath their workaday life, you will find a fascinating history. Outside the towns, amongst the patchwork of fields and alarmingly narrow lanes, are some of Devon's prettiest villages, such as Sheepwash and Winkleigh – and one or two surprises.

BICKLEIGH Map ref SS9407

Bickleigh is a pretty village of thatched cottages on either side of the River Exe linked by a narrow 300-year-old bridge, reputedly the inspiration for Paul Simon's song *Bridge over Troubled Water*. Close by the bridge is Devonshire's Country Living Centre, the watermill has been converted into a craft centre with workshops.

Just outside the village, off the Crediton road, is Bickleigh Castle, a fortified manor house which has a

Stately Fursdon has retained its poise, despite the ravages of fortune

The gatehouse of historic Bickleigh Castle dates from the 15th century and includes a fine armoury

KING OF THE GYPSIES
The Carews were certainly not a dull family, but the most notorious of all must be Bampfylde Moore Carew, who was born into an advantaged life, but went off the rails in a spectacular way. While he was still a schoolboy, at the famous Blundell's School in Tiverton, he fell in with a band of gypsies and ran away to lead the life of a Romany. A born leader and accomplished confidence trickster, he eventually became the King of the Gypsies and tales of his exploits have become legendary. Bampfylde is buried in an unmarked grave in the churchyard at Bickleigh.

fascinating history. The fortunes of the castle and its various occupants have been mixed, to say the least. In the early 16th century it came into the ownership of the Carews, after the runaway marriage of Elizabeth Courtenay, granddaughter of the Earl of Devon, and Thomas Carew, the younger brother of her guardian. Another Carew, Sir George, was in command of the ill-fated *Mary Rose*, Henry VIII's flagship which sank in the Solent. For the family's Royalist sympathies during the Civil War, the greater part of the castle was demolished, but the restored gatehouse, the ancient chapel and the cob and thatch farmhouse, which the family then occupied, can be visited. Restored at the beginning of the 20th century, the various buildings form a delightful complex which bears witness to the many centuries which have passed since the castle was first built. Bickleigh is at the mid-point of the Exe Valley Way, a long-distance route which follows this lovely valley from Exmoor to the estuary at Falmouth.

A little further from Bickleigh, also off the Crediton road, is Fursdon House, the home of one of Devon's oldest families since the 13th century, though the present house is only 400 years old. It contains historic costumes, mementoes, archives and portraits.

COBBATON Map ref SS6126
Within a maze of lanes, south east of Barnstaple, is one of the most surprising attractions in the whole county, the Cobbaton Combat Collection. Crammed into two large exhibition halls is a vast collection of military vehicles, guns, weapons and other equipment from all over the world. You can walk in amongst them and peer into them; some are arranged as tableaux, depicting how they would have been used. This private collection is the result of the obsession of one man, Preston Isaac, who began amassing militaria of all kinds over 40 years ago. There are exhibits from World War II and the Warsaw Pact countries, as well as reference displays on World War I, the Falklands conflict and the Gulf War. One of

the more recent acquisitions is a Chieftain tank from Checkpoint Charlie in Berlin. Reconstructions of civilian wartime scenes feature in the Home Front displays and the exhibition halls resound with the sounds of Glen Miller, The Andrews Sisters and recorded news items. The theme of this fascinating collection never wavers – the children's play area has a Sherman tank to clamber over and refreshments are served from a NAAFI wagon.

CREDITON Map ref SS8300

This is a pleasant and attractive town and though many of its historically important buildings have gone, destroyed by a series of fires over the years, there remains an air of former glory about the place. This becomes most apparent when the parish church comes into view – a huge and impressive building of cathedral proportions. The fact is that there was once a cathedral here, and Crediton's distinguished history is largely based upon its religious heritage. It all started in AD 680 when a child, christened Winfrith, was born here. He grew up to become one of the greatest of Christian missionaries, one of the founding fathers of the Christian Church in Europe and patron saint of both Germany and The Netherlands – St Boniface.

The first diocesan church was built here in AD 909 and served as a cathedral until 1050, when the bishopric was moved to Exeter. The present building has some Norman parts, but mostly dates from around 1410. Though no longer a cathedral, the collegiate church was so important to the townspeople that when Henry VIII dissolved it in 1547, they negotiated its purchase for £300 and set up a board of twelve governors to control its affairs, and this practice has survived to this day.

ON PARADE
Crediton's Belle Parade gets is name from the period between 1805 and 1812, when French naval prisoners of war, resplendent in their blue and yellow uniforms, were allowed to parade here.

CREDITON'S HERMIT
One of Crediton's ancient buildings is the chapel of St Lawrence off Threshers Road at the western end of the High Street. Built in about 1200, it included a cell for a religious hermit, who would dispense counsel to those who came to him for advice. The building has been restored, but the two end walls are original.

Credited with bringing Christianity to Germany, the missionary St Boniface is commemorated in the town

A SCENIC ROUTE
By far the best approach to Crediton is along the A3072 from Bickleigh. This switchback road passes through some of Devon's loveliest countryside and offers one breathtaking view after another.

TARKA COUNTRY
Great Torrington overlooks the Torridge and its tributaries – *Tarka the Otter* country. There are still otters here, but in much fewer numbers than in Henry Williamson's day, and visitors are unlikely to see the shy, mostly nocturnal creatures in the wild. If you do want to see otters, there is an Otter Trust sanctuary over the border in Cornwall, at North Petherwin near Launceston (about 25 miles/40km from Barnstaple). Asian otters (related to our own variety) can be seen at Combe Martin Wildlife Park and at the Dartmoor Otter Sanctuary at Buckfastleigh.

The main square of Great Torrington is a bustling local centre

Before the mid-19th century there were no shops in Crediton's High Street, everything was bought from stalls set up along the middle of the road. These markets originated in 1231, and from 1306 until fairly recently a cattle fair was held each spring, the largest of its kind in the West Country, with the High Street, then the new cattle market, full of the distinctive Red Devon breed.

GREAT TORRINGTON   Map ref SS4919
If the approach to Torrington seems rather dull, don't be disheartened because this is a delightful little town with a great deal to see and do. Turn off the unappealing through-road into the town centre and you will discover the heart of the place – a charming square which is most people's idea of what a real town centre should be. There is a lovely old inn which has Civil War connections, a fine Town Hall and a Market Hall, and just around the corner from the square, The Plough Arts Centre has a lively programme of entertainment.

Torrington is set high on a hill overlooking lush agricultural land, on three sides it has common land, preserved by Act of Parliament, and below it flows the wide River Torridge. The Dartington Crystal factory was established in the town in the 1960s, when Swedish craftsmen were brought here to train a local workforce in the art of glass-blowing. The company rapidly expanded, exporting its fine crystal all over the world, but its operation here is very much geared to its large number of visitors. The factory tours are fascinating, and high walkways enable visitors to look down over the teams of craftsmen and witness their glass-blowing skills. Every stage in the production, from furnace to packing case, can be seen and there is a very good video introduction and a display of glassware in the entrance hall. After the tour there is, of course, the opportunity to buy, from a vast showroom. Another showroom sells pottery, gift items and kitchenware, and there is an airy cafeteria.

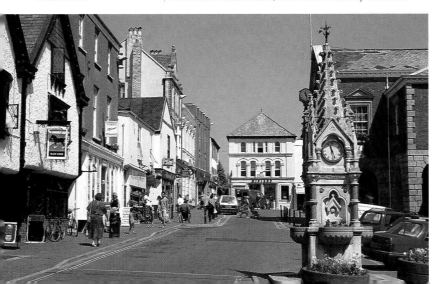

Just south of the town on the B3220 Exeter road, Rosemoor Gardens have long been famous and are continuing to expand and develop new areas of cultivation. The original eight acres were created by Lady Anne Barry to surround her home, but in 1988 she gave them, along with a further 32 acres of land, to the Royal Horticultural Society who have wasted no time in making full use of the opportunity afforded to them. A National Garden is being created here, and the previously uncultivated land has now been planted with a number of gardens. There are two rose gardens containing around 2,000 roses in 200 varieties, wonderful herbaceous borders, colour-theme gardens, a herb garden and potager, an extensive stream and bog garden centred on an ornamental lake, a cottage garden and a foliage garden. Fruit and vegetable cultivation has not been left out and exciting new developments are always under way. There is a good visitor centre with a restaurant and shop, as well as plants for sale, many propagated from specimens in the gardens.

HATHERLEIGH Map ref SS5404

If you approach Hatherleigh from the north you will be entering the lovely little market town the best way, on the road which twists and turns down a steep hillside lined with pretty colour-washed cottages and ancient pubs, including the lovely Tally Ho Inn, which has its own brewery. If you approach Hatherleigh at all on a Tuesday morning, be prepared to do it slowly because you will probably be behind a string of farmers heading for the market in anything from a large modern cattle truck to an old estate car with a couple of sheep in the back! All local life converges on Hatherleigh on market day, and a couple of hours wandering around the market and the town beats any organised tourist attraction. The poultry auction is particularly entertaining, and the little cheese shop has a wonderful variety of cheeses, including local ones. The town itself has antiques and junk shops and its own pottery on the main street.

THE MID TORRIDGE CYCLE LINK
This attractive route links the Tarka Trail cycle/walkway (see page 44) at Petrockstowe, with the Sticklepath cycle route (see page 72) as it passes through Hatherleigh on its way to Dartmoor. These three cycle trails, when combined, form a continuous route from Dartmoor to the north Devon coast.

TEAMWORK
The organised, almost choreographed, way in which the glass-blowers at Dartington Crystal interact makes compulsive viewing. Without a word or a glance, they cross and re-cross each others paths as they move backwards and forwards from furnace to workplace, passing the hot glass from place to place for each stage of the process in what appear to the uninitiated to be a series of near-disaster situations.

Pastel-washed buildings in the unspoilt market town of Hatherleigh

Taw Valley and the Tarka Trail

A not-too-energetic walk along well-waymarked paths through Forestry Commission plantations and following a scenic stretch of the Tarka Trail.

Time: Approx. 2½ hours. Distance: 4 miles (6.4km).
Location: 10 miles (16.1km) northwest of Crediton.
Start: Eggesford Wood Forestry Commission Car Park, off the A377.
(OS grid ref: SS694705.)
OS Map: Explorer 127 (South Molton & Chulmleigh) 1:25,000.
See Key to Walks on page 121.

ROUTE DIRECTIONS

From the parking area (toilets, information point) follow the 'Forest Walks' sign to the 'Start Walks' post. Turn left and almost immediately right uphill following red markers. Continue on this path as it turns along the woodland edge and descends to a broad track. Turn right on the track, then turn left downhill on a waymarked path parallel with a brook and continue, disregarding the red-marked trail to the left, to the A377.

Cross the road and stile opposite, then bear diagonally left through a meadow (can be waterlogged) to a stile and pass beneath the railway. Follow the well-arrowed path and shortly climb steps and cross the River Taw beside the railway. Descend steps, pass through a kissing gate, bear right up through another gate and gently climb to merge with a wide grassy track. Keep right to a gate and shortly bear right on to a gravel track – the **Tarka Trail**.

Pass through a gate beside **Eggesford** church and proceed along the now metalled lane, with the ruins of Eggesford House in view on the hill ahead, to a lane beyond Eggesford Gardens County Centre. Turn right and very soon turn left at a junction signed 'Wembworthy'.

Proceed up the lane to a coniferous plantation on your left. Climb the stile on its fringe and follow the established path through the woodland, passing two **commemorative stones** to a crossroads of tracks. Turn left and go through a gate on to a blue-arrowed bridleway between farm buildings.

Keep ahead where the track

Eggesford church, built to serve the spiritual needs of the Chichester family, lies marooned

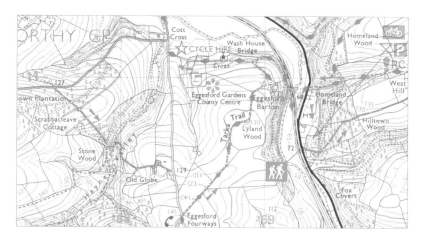

bears right into Scrabbacleave House and descend to a gate and enter woodland (can be muddy). On reaching a forest track in Hayne Valley, go straight across and descend a path to a stone bridge. Beyond the bridge, the path soon bears left, then right uphill through the trees. At a fork on the woodland edge, keep ahead to a gate, then bear left at the next junction and soon pass through Old Globe Farm to reach a lane.

Turn right, follow the lane into Eggesford Fourways, and just before the memorial cross turn left through a waymarked gate to rejoin the Tarka Trail. Proceed along a track (can be muddy) with splendid views across the Taw Valley and rolling farmland. Follow the track left beside a barn, climb a stile flanking a gate, then keep to the field edge to access the track from Eggesford Barton Farm.

Turn left and shortly turn right on to a grassy track and retrace your steps back across the River Taw, beneath the railway and across the A377. Back in Eggesford Wood, turn right across the brook by wooden railings and follow a red-marked trail to the tarmac road to return to the car park.

POINTS OF INTEREST

The Tarka Trail

With a theme taken from Henry Williamson's classic novel *Tarka the Otter*, this 180-mile (288-km) long-distance route allows walkers to explore the places that Tarka visited on his journeys. The trail passes through many different landscapes, ranging from the high moors of Dartmoor and Exmoor, through the wooded Taw and Torridge valleys to the rugged north Devon coast.

Eggesford

Nestling in a peaceful spot Eggesford's church of All Saints stands isolated in the former grounds of Eggesford House. Dating from the late 14th century, the church is noted for a magnificent memorial, commissioned in 1650 by Lord Chichester, to his two wives.

Originally standing near the church and once the seat of the Chichester family (ancestors of the round-the-world sailor Sir Francis Chichester), Eggesford House was demolished in 1832 and an impressive mansion built on the hill, west of the church, by the

Earl of Portsmouth. It was sold in 1917 and has since fallen into decay.

The Eggesford Gardens County Centre provides information on places to visit in the area.

Commemorative Stones

The Forestry Commission was formed in 1919 and much of the woodland was acquired from Eggesford Estate. The first tree planting by the Commission was carried out on 8 December 1919 and the first plaque commemorates that occasion. The second marks its 50th anniversary.

Otters were a more common sight along the River Torridge in 1927, when Williamson's popular novel appeared

Quince Honey Farm, one of the many attractions of South Molton

SWEET WORDS

Bees and honey have figured largely in literature, history and mythology. The Greek gods on Mount Olympus drank a kind of honey (nectar) and references to honey occur many times in the Bible, usually in metaphoric phrases concerning all the good things in life – as in 'A land flowing with milk and honey'. Poets were also fond of the stuff – particularly Rupert Brooke, who evoked the English rural idyll with:

> *'Stands the church clock at ten to three?*
> *And is there honey still for tea?'.*

But the greatest literary eulogist on the delights of honey is, of course, A A Milne's Winnie the Pooh.

SOUTH MOLTON Map ref SS7125

Once on the main holiday route to the north coast, South Molton, now free of through traffic, is a delightful little town. In spite of the very grand Town Hall and the antiques shops, craft and art galleries, it is still a working town, with supermarkets, banks, bakers' shops and the like. By no means 'touristy', South Molton nevertheless has a variety of attractions, including Quince Honey Farm. Established in 1949, this is Britain's largest honey farm, and its work is illustrated with a very good video and with hives full of bees. About 20 different kinds of habitat have been set up behind glass, and the innovative design of the exhibition hives enable visitors to open them at the press of a button to show the bees living and working inside. A variety of honey and beeswax products are on sale in an extensive shop area.

THE TARKA TRAIL

Most people know of Tarka the Otter, the subject of that wonderful book (and subsequent film) by Henry Williamson, and it was during his sojourn here in the 1920s that Williamson found his inspiration when he became the adoptive 'parent' of an orphaned otter cub.

These days Tarka is everywhere, giving his name to teashops and guesthouses as well as a long-distance trail through the countryside which his creator wrote about. The trail is based as far as possible on the route taken by Tarka along the rivers Taw and Torridge and extends for 180 miles (288km) from Dartmoor to Exmoor and the north coast, with access points along the way (see Walk on page 42). Over 30 miles (48km) are on the trackbeds of disused railway lines and these are designated cycleways. The part between Barnstaple and Great Torrington forms the Tarka Country Park, and horse-riding is allowed between Torrington and Petrockstowe.

TIVERTON Map ref SS9512

For a town to prosper these days, its proximity to the
motorway network is of considerable importance; in the
old days it was the rivers that provided the lifeline.
Tiverton, with its two rivers, the Grand Western Canal
and the M5 just a short distance away, has always been
advantaged and it remains a lively centre for the
surrounding area. The appearance of the town today
owes much to the prosperity of its textile and clothing
industries in the 16th and 17th centuries, when rich
wool merchants endowed their town with such splendid
buildings as St Peter's Church, Blundell's School, the
Great House and three sets of almshouses. St George's
Church, built in 1773, is believed to be one of the finest
Georgian churches in Devon.

Tiverton's history is well documented in the excellent
town museum, in St Andrew Street, which includes a
Heathcoat Lace Gallery, an agricultural section, two
waterwheels and a railway gallery.

Tiverton's two rivers are the Exe and the Lowman
(Tiverton means 'two ford town'), and the former is
overlooked by Tiverton Castle. Dating from 1106, the
castle was originally moated on three sides, with the Exe
on the fourth, but all that remains of the original
building is one circular tower.

Just north of Tiverton is Knightshayes Court, an
ornate 19th-century mansion built for Sir John
Heathcoat-Amory, whose fortune came from the lace
industry. Designed by William Burges, it features rich
Gothic-style decoration, painted ceilings and wall
stencilling. The house is more than equally matched by
the wonderful grounds that surround it, comprising a
pleasing mixture of formal gardens, woodland and
ornamental shrubs.

THE GRAND WESTERN

The system of canals known as
The Grand Western was
originally intended to link the
Bristol Channel and the
English Channel, but for
financial reasons the scheme
never reached completion –
the parts from Taunton to
Burlescombe and the branch
to Tiverton are all that were
built. After the railway came
to Tiverton in the 1840s, the
canal declined, but it was
rescued and restored during
the 1960s, becoming a
country park where the
tranquil surroundings and
wildlife can be enjoyed.
Horse-drawn boat trips are
also available from the canal
basin in Tiverton.

*St Peter's Church, its tower
soaring above the River Exe,
was raised by Tiverton's
prosperous wool merchants*

Through the Heart of Rural Devon

A gently undulating and possibly muddy ramble along field paths, woodland tracks and peaceful country lanes, in a very rural and unspoilt part of mid-Devon.

Time: Approx. 3½ hours. Distance: 6 miles (9.7km).
Location: 4 miles (6.4km) northwest of Hatherleigh.
Start: Sheepwash village square. (OS grid ref: SS486063.)
OS Maps: Explorer 112 (Launceston & Holsworthy)
1:25,000.
Explorer 126 (Clovelly & Hartland)
1;25,000.
See Key to Walks on page 121.

ROUTE DIRECTIONS

From the square in **Sheepwash** take the lane past the post office, signed 'St Petrockstowe'. Leave the village confines and continue ahead passing farm buildings on the right to an arrowed path left through a gate. Keep to the right-hand hedge, through three fields to a stile and trackway. Cross straight over and go down the field, with a hedge right, and over a footbridge.

Proceed uphill (signed with a yellow arrow), pass through a signed gate past a barn and on up a track to a gate and a lane. Cross the lane to join a grass-centred track, which soon bears left, then right, down to Lake Farm. Keep on the track past a barn and the entrance to Blackmoat Farm to descend past the complex of buildings at Buckland Mill. At a fingerpost, bear left, follow the track right beside the mill leat, and in a few yards cross the bridge over Mussel Brook.

At a junction of tracks, keep right and continue through Buckland Wood, finally reaching a lane. Turn left and continue ahead to eventually enter **Buckland Filleigh**. Bear left with fingerpost along the driveway towards Buckland House (school) and church. On nearing the house follow yellow arrows left, then right, and pass through the lychgate into the churchyard.

Turn left at the porch, following the tarmac path to a stile, then bear right downhill through parkland to cross a footbridge near the lake. Ascend beside a clump of trees then bear right along a track towards a house visible in the trees.

Go through a gate, turn left along a lane, then in about half a mile (0.8km) at a sharp right-hand bend by a house, bear left through a waymarked kissing gate and almost immediately right on a signed footpath through coniferous woodland. Enter a field, keep to the left-hand edge and continue into the next field, soon to cross a stile on your left.

Bear diagonally right across a field and join a track in the corner leading to a lane. Turn left and shortly right through Upcott Barton farmyard to a

Bright geraniums stand by the door of a cosily thatched house in Sheepwash

group of dilapidated buildings. The right-hand one is a former **chapel**, go through the gate on the right then turn left and proceed downhill keeping close to the right-hand edge, until the hedge turns away right, then ahead to a stream and footbridge.

Cross the footbridge, climb a stile on the fringe of the copse and head uphill for a short distance, parallel with a brook through a gap in the hedge. Bear right following the old hedge and soon join a track leading down to a gate and brook. Stay on this green lane back into Sheepwash, bearing right on the village lane to reach the square.

POINTS OF INTEREST

Sheepwash
The name of this sleepy, unspoilt cluster of houses, nestling near the River Torridge, comes from the days when farmers washed their sheep in the river.

Virtually unchanged since the 18th century, the four picturesque streets converge on a central square, which boasts a fine inn, the parish church, thatched and colour-washed cob cottages, the village pump and an old chestnut tree.

In the 17th century there were stepping stones across the river, but after a villager's son was drowned the father paid for a bridge to be built. He also donated money for its upkeep and the Bridgeland Trust was formed. Today the Trust helps the church and the elderly in the village.

Buckland Filleigh
This tiny hamlet is dominated by Buckland

House which is used as a school. The attractive little church beside it overlooks open parkland.

Upcott Barton
Upcott Barton farm lies on an old settlement and the interesting old building, now used for storage, was once a chapel, as the shaped windows indicate.

Devon's Rural Heartland

Leisure Information

Places of Interest

Shopping

The Performing Arts

Sports, Activities and the Outdoors

Checklist

Annual Events and Customs

Leisure Information

TOURIST INFORMATION CENTRES

Crediton
Old Town Hall, High Street.
Tel: 01363 772006.
South Molton
Information Centre, 1 East
Street. Tel: 01769 574122.
Limited winter opening.
Tiverton
Phoenix Lane. Tel: 01884
255827.

OTHER INFORMATION

Devon Wildlife Trust
Shirehampton House, 35–37 St
David's Hill, Exeter. Tel: 01392
279244.
English Heritage
29 Queen Square, Bristol.
Tel: 0117 975 0700.
www.english-heritage.org.uk
Forest Enterprise England
340 Bristol Business Park,
Coldharbour Lane, Bristol.
Tel: 0117 906 6000.
National Trust for Devon
Killerton House, Broadclyst,
Exeter. Tel: 01392 881691.
www.nationaltrust.org.uk
English Nature Devonteam
Level 2 Renslade House, Bonhay
Road, Exeter. Tel: 01392 88970.
South West Lakes Trust
Highercombe Park, Lewdown,

Okehampton. Tel: 01837
871565.

ORDNANCE SURVEY MAPS

Explorer 1:25,000. Sheets 112,
113, 114, 126, 127.
Landranger 1:50,000. Sheets
180, 181, 191, 192.

Places of Interest

Unless otherwise stated, there
will be an admission charge to
the following places of interest.
Bickleigh Castle
Tel: 01884 855363. Open Easter
to early Oct, most days.
**Cobbaton Combat
Collection**
Cobbaton, Chittlehampton.
Tel: 01769 540740/540414.
Open all year daily, most days in
winter.
Dartington Crystal
Great Torrington. Tel: 01805
626244. Open all year, most
days.
Fursdon House
Cadbury, Thorverton. Tel:
01392 860860. Open BHs &
Wed, Thu pm Jun–Aug.
Knightshayes Court
Knightshayes Court. Tel: 01884
254665. Open end Mar–early
Oct, most days.
Quince Honey Farm
South Molton. Tel: 01769

572401. Open early Apr–Oct
daily.
Rosemoor Gardens
Great Torrington. Tel: 01805
624067. Open Apr–Sep.
Tiverton Castle
Tiverton. Tel: 01884 253200.
Open Jul & Aug most days,
limited opening Apr–Jun & Sep.
Tiverton Museum
Beck's Square. Tel: 01884
256295. Open Feb–Christmas,
daily except Sun.

SPECIAL INTEREST FOR CHILDREN

The following places may be of
interest to visitors with children.
Unless otherwise stated, there
will be an admission charge.
Devon Badger Watch
5 miles (8km) north of Tiverton.
Tel: 01398 351506. Fully-lit
viewing of badger sett, above
and below ground. Open
May–Oct, most evenings
(booking essential).
North Devon Farm Park
Marsh Farm, Landkey. Tel:
01271 830255. Open Apr–Oct,
limited winter opening.

Shopping

Hatherleigh
Antiques, crafts and galleries.
Cattle market Tue.

South Molton
Antiques and crafts
Pannier Market Thu and Sat,
livestock Thu.
Holsworthy
Open air market Wed; livestock
Wed and Thu.
Tiverton
Market Tue, Fri and Sat.

LOCAL SPECIALITIES

Cider
Gray's Farm Cider, Halstow,
Tedburn St Mary. Tel: 01647
61236.
Palmerhayes Devon Cider &
Scrumpy. Tel: 01884 254579.
Clotted Cream
Many shops send cream by post.
Crafts
Devonshire's Country Living
Centre, Bickleigh Mill, Bickleigh.
Tel: 01884 855419.
Tiverton Craft Centre, 1 Bridge
Street, West Exe, Tiverton.
Tel: 01844 258430. Pottery,
basket work, wood craft and
slate work.
Glass
The Dartington Crystal Visitor
Centre, Great Torrington.
Tel: 01805 626269.
**Honey, Candles and
Beeswax**
Quince Honey Farm, South
Molton. Tel: 01769 572401.
Pottery
Barton Pottery, South Barton,
Canonsleigh, Burlescombe,
Tiverton. Tel: 01823 672987.
Hatherleigh Pottery, 20 Market
Street, Hatherleigh. Tel: 01837
810624.
Monkleigh Pottery, Monkleigh,
nr Bideford. Tel: 01805 623194.
Wine
Yearlstone Vineyard, Bickleigh,
Tiverton. Tel: 01884 855700.

The Performing Arts

Plough Arts Centre
Great Torrington, live music,
theatre and films. Tel: 01805
622552.

Sports, Activities and the Outdoors

ANGLING

Fly
Bellbrook Valley Trout Fishery

Bellbrook Farm, Oakford,
Tiverton. Tel: 01398 351292.
Book in advance.
Coarse
Creedy Lake, Long Barn,
Crediton. Tel: 01363 772684.
Grand Western Canal, Tiverton.
Day and season tickets from
local tackle shops.
Oaktree Fishery, Yeo Mill, West
Anstey, South Molton. Tel:
01398 341568.
Salmon Hutch Coarse Fishery,
Uton, Crediton.
Tel: 01363 772749.
No closed season. Suitable for
disabled.

BOAT TRIPS

Grand Western Horseboat Co,
The Wharf, Canal Hill, Tiverton.
Horsedrawn barge along the
Grand Western Canal.
Tel: 01884 253345.

COUNTRY PARKS, FORESTS AND NATURE RESERVES

Abbeyford Woods. Tel: 01409
221692.
Eggesford Forest. Tel: 01392
832262.
Grand Western Canal Country
Park, Tiverton. Tel: 01884
254072.

CYCLING

For information about cycle
routes in the area – The Tarka
Trail, Mid Torridge Cycle Link –
contact the local Tourist
Information Centres. Also visit
www.devon.gov.uk/tourism/ncn

CYCLE HIRE

Great Torrington
Torridge Cycle Hire, The Station.
Tel: 01805 622633.
Tiverton
Maynards Cycle Shop, 25 Gold
Street.
Tel: 01884 253979.

GOLF COURSES

Chulmleigh
Chulmleigh Golf Club, Leigh
Road. Tel: 01769 580519.
Crediton
Downes Crediton Golf Club.
Tel: 01363 773025.
Tedburn St Mary
Fingle Glen Family Golf Centre.
Tel: 01647 61817.

Tiverton
Tiverton Golf Club, Post Hill.
Tel: 01884 252187.

HORSE-RIDING

Calverleigh
Rose and Crown Riding Stables,
Palmer's Lodge. Tel: 01884
252060.
Chulmleigh
Bold Try Equestrian Centre,
Leigh Road. Tel: 01769 580366.
Cullompton
Heazle Riding Centre,
Clayhidon. Tel: 01823 680280.

SHOOTING

Uton
Crediton Gun Club. Tel: 01363
773537.
Tiverton
Tiverton Small Bore Rifle Club.
Tel: 01884 252268.

Annual Events and Customs

Crediton
Boniface Festival, early June.
South Molton
Olde English Fayre, mid-
September.
Tiverton
Spring Festival, May.
Mid Devon Show, July.

The checklists give details of just
some of the facilities within the
area covered by this guide.
Further information can be
obtained from Tourist
Information Centres.

*Country pursuits celebrated
on a Hatherleigh inn sign*

Dartmoor and The Tamar Valley

Dartmoor is southern England's last great wilderness, though you might not think so if you only visit the picturesque villages of Widecombe or Buckland, set among gentle, rolling hills. But the bracken- and heather-covered uplands, interrupted by stark and distinctive granite outcrops, is quite another world, with mysterious standing stones dating back at least 6,000 years. Medieval tin, lead and copper miners have also left their mark. The Tamar Valley is an area of outstanding natural beauty, and if you take to the water, either along the Tamar itself, or on a trip around Plymouth Sound you will get so much more out of it.

DARTMOOR LETTERBOXES
The first 'Dartmoor letterbox' was established just over 5 miles (8km) northwest of Postbridge at Cranmere Pool, a peat bog which, in 1854, was virtually inaccessible. Someone had the idea of putting a bottle here so those who had made it could leave a calling card. Serious walkers responded in their droves. In 1894 another 'letterbox' site appeared; clues and map references were given as to its location, and so a fad was born. Since then there have been several variations on the 'calling card' theme but today, over 4,000 letterboxes later, a rubber stamp and inkpad provides proof of visit. Any Dartmoor tourist information office will tell you how to search for letterboxes.

ASHBURTON   Map ref SX7570

Ashburton is the largest settlement on Dartmoor, though with just 3,500 inhabitants it is hardly a metropolis. It is a handsome, well-to-do market town with several fine old gabled and slate-hung houses, but the most important building is the 15th-century church, a monument to the profits of tin and cloth for which the town was once famous. During the tin boom Ashburton was one of Devon's four Stannary Towns (see Tavistock page 73) and Ashburton cloth even found its way to China. In later years iron mining added to the town's coffers. Today Ashburton still basks in its former prosperity and although visitors pass through here, stopping in the fine old pubs or browsing in antiques shops, the town does not rely heavily on tourism.

There is a local museum in the town centre, with a good collection of native American artefacts, but the main attraction in this area is the family-oriented River Dart Country Park, towards Holne, with woodland and riverside walks, adventure playground and a lake.

BOVEY TRACEY   Map ref SX8178

Bovey Tracey is a pleasant small market town which bills itself as the Gateway to Dartmoor, because of its location at the busy southeastern corner of the moor. It is definitely worth a stop to explore the woodland and riverside walks of the Parke Estate (National Trust), half a mile (0.8km) west of the town.

Back in the centre of Bovey Tracey is the beautifully restored Riverside Mill building – never actually used as a mill. It was built in 1850 as stables and the waterwheel simply scooped water from the river to a cistern used by the stables and adjacent house. It now houses a showcase for the 240 members of the Devon Guild of Craftsmen, who produce some of the finest contemporary arts and crafts in the country, including jewellery, textiles, prints, ceramics and furniture.

Near by is the Teign Valley Glass and House of Marbles centre, a large shop situated in the former Bovey Tracey Pottery buildings selling all manner of marbles, glassware, games and toys. This is a major wet-weather attraction but the real interest is in the free demonstrations of glass-blowing. Three museums on the site explain the history of the Bovey potteries, glass, board games and marbles.

Near Bovey Tracey are a number of tors – naturally formed granite rock towers, often weathered into strange shapes by the forces of erosion. Haytor Rocks is the most accessible; the 30-feet (9m) high Bowerman's Nose is the most curiously shaped, resembling a face in profile. According to one local legend, it is a local man who defied the injunction to rest on the Sabbath, went out hunting and was turned to stone; another has it that he disturbed a coven of witches who subsequently petrified him and his hounds (Hound Tor). Near by lies the Hound Tor Deserted Medieval Village, the scant remains of dwellings, stables and grain stores of farmsteads which were inhabited from the Bronze Age to around 1300.

THE INFAMOUS WILLIAM DE TRACEY

The Tracey in Bovey Tracey comes from a Norman family who settled here after the Conquest. Its most infamous member, William de Tracey, was one of the knights who slew Thomas à Becket in Canterbury Cathedral in 1170. It is said that he rebuilt the town's beautiful church of SS Peter, Paul and Thomas as penance for his part in the murder. The present church dates mainly from the 14th and 15th centuries and is famous for its coloured screen.

The weathered rocks of Haytor resemble some ancient beast in battle

Becka Falls and The Bovey Valley

A waymarked walk on defined paths and nature trails, through mixed woodland in the Bovey Valley Woodlands Nature Reserve, and beside the tumbling Becka Brook. There is one steady climb and descent on uneven stony paths which can be very wet after prolonged rain.

Time: Approx. 2½ hours. Distance: 4 miles (6.4km).
Location: 4½ miles (7.2km) northwest of Bovey Tracey.
Start: Manaton village car park, near green on unclassified road.
(OS grid ref: SX750812.)
OS Maps: Outdoor Leisure 28 (Dartmoor)1:25,000.
See Key to Walks on page 121.

ROUTE DIRECTIONS

Leave the car park in **Manaton** by the car entrance at the crossroads and cross to the lane, signed 'Leighon'. Go down the lane past Mill Farm and ascend to Hayne Cross. Turn left, and in about half a mile (0.8km) reach a crossroads at Kestor Inn. Turn right on the main road passing houses on your left and take the path left through a gate.

Bear right following the path close to the woodland edge, soon entering the wood. Keep on the main path, ignoring all side paths, to a stile. Cross and follow the yellow waymarks to a wooden bridge. Continue up steps, signed 'To the Falls' and at a fork take steps down right to visit the base of **Becka Falls**. Return to fork and continue on the main path (still with yellow waymarks) over a stile and in 300 yards (274m) reach a junction of paths.

Proceed straight ahead, signed 'Bovey Valley for Lustleigh' and after a further 300 yards (274m) at a fork turn left and immediately left again up a narrow path past **Bovey Valley Woodlands Nature Reserve** information board to the top of the hill. Descend steeply through the rich woodland to meet a bridleway and a wall.

Turn left through the old gateway and climb steadily up the wooded valley eventually reaching a narrow track. Continue along this through a gate, then keep right to reach a crossing of paths at the top of the valley, close to the hamlet of Water and an old watermill. Turn right, signed 'Manaton indirect' along a track through Letchole Plantation with good cameo

A neatly thatched row of holiday cottages in Manaton

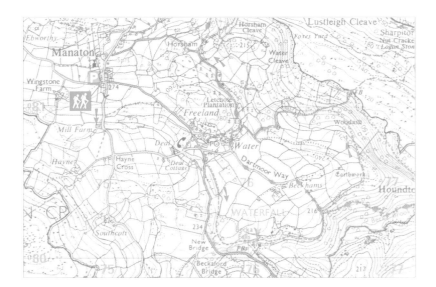

views across the Bovey Valley.

At a junction of paths by a garage (Horsham) turn left uphill beside a brook, signed 'Manaton', and gradually ascend, passing through two gates to a lane. Turn left passing Manaton village hall, and cross the village green to the car park.

POINTS OF INTEREST

Manaton

The most attractive part of this scattered hamlet is the cluster of buildings nestling around the green and parish church at Upper Manaton. St Winifred's Church dates from the 15th century and features a fine carved rood screen that extends right across the building.

Close to the church is Wingstone Farm, which was the home of the novelist John Galsworthy between 1904 and 1924. He created the Forsyte family whose popular sagas have become a part of literary and television history.

Near the village on the open moorland is Hound Tor, where there is a medieval settlement of long houses inhabited from Saxon times to AD 1300 and excavated in 1961.

Becka Falls

Best seen after heavy rain, these falls (also known as Becky Falls) are created by the picturesque Becka Brook as it leaps and plunges 70 feet (21m) down a series of great boulders. There is a café and visitor centre near the falls, and the nearby oak woodland is carpeted with wild flowers in springtime.

Bovey Valley Woodlands Nature Reserve

The reserve is predominantly semi-natural oak and hazel woodland, lying in a deep valley carved out of Dartmoor granite along a geological fault. Stretching over 2½ miles (4km), the valley contains one of the largest areas of oak woodland in the Dartmoor National Park. It provides a haven for a wide variety of animals and insects, including the protected dormouse and the high brown fritillary butterfly. Riverside boulders and trees are covered with rare mosses and lichens. Some of the more unusual birds to look out for are the dipper, grey wagtail, wood warbler and summer migrants like the pied flycatcher and redstart.

The pied flycatcher is a summer visitor to Devon

The little church at Brent Tor stands exposed on the hilltop, providing an excellent viewpoint

ST MICHAEL AT BRENT TOR
A description of the Church of St Michael at Brent Tor taken from a Survey of Devon by Risdon in 1630:
   'A church full bleak and weather beaten, all alone as it were forsaken, whose churchyard doth hardly afford depth of earth to bury the dead'

BRENT TOR   Map ref SX4780

The tiny church of St Michael at Brent Tor, a mile (1.6km) southwest of North Brentor village, is dramatically elevated 1,100 feet (335m) above sea level on a small, steep volcanic (plug) hillock. On a clear day, views stretch as far as Plymouth Sound to the south and some 40 miles (64km) northwards to the hills of Exmoor. But look around and there is nothing, so why was a church built here? There are the usual Dartmoor tales relating to mischief by the devil, but a more plausible theory is that the tor may have been the only land visible to a 12th-century seafarer in distress. He vowed that should he survive he would dedicate a church on that particular spot, and so in 1130 Brent Tor was built. Today's church, mostly from the 15th century but restored in the 19th century, has walls just 10 feet (3m) tall, but to survive the fearsome elemental lashing they receive they were built 3 feet (1m) thick from the same volcanic material as the tor.

BUCKFASTLEIGH   Map ref SX7366

The old market town of Buckfastleigh lies in a lush wooded valley, bypassed by the A38 and by most visitors who head for either the station or Buckfast Abbey. The station is home to the South Devon Valley Railway, a gloriously nostalgic steam line which runs along a beautiful 7-mile (11.2-km) stretch of the River Dart as far as Totnes. The station site is shared by the excellent Buckfast Butterflies and Dartmoor Otter Sanctuary. The former is a large 'rain forest' hot house where exotic rainbow-hued specimens have no qualms about gently landing on visitors (a sort of 'wings-on' experience!). The Otter Sanctuary is a quasi-natural habitat with unobtrusive observation points where you can watch these graceful creatures swim and play. Both are serious conservation projects, successfully walking the thin line between entertainment and education.

There are more animals to see at Pennywell, an 80-acre farm and wildlife centre a mile (1.6km) to the south which scores particularly well with its long list of daily events which include bottle-feeding, hand-milking, falconry demonstrations, sheepdog trials, pony training, ferret racing and even 'worm charming'.

If you do eventually make it into the centre of Buckfastleigh, brave the 196 cobbled steps which climb up on the northeast side of town (near the car park) to the church. This fine 13th-century monument was sadly destroyed by fire in 1992 but it's well worth coming up here for the views over the surrounding countryside. Immediately below your feet the limestone hillside is dotted with caves.

BUCKFAST ABBEY Map ref SX7467

Buckfast Abbey is one of the wonders of 20th-century England. The magnificent Abbey Church is a huge, austere mix of Early English and Norman styles, completed between 1906 and 1937. There's nothing remarkable in that until you learn that just four monks built it and only one of them had any prior experience of masonry work. Were the abbey to acquire a veneer of age it would certainly be indistinguishable from its medieval forebear.

Today a community of 42 monks lead a life of prayer, work and study, not dissimilar to their counterparts who lived here from 1018 until the Dissolution in 1539. The monks returned in 1882, discovered the ruined medieval foundations and began the monumental task of totally rebuilding monastery and church. Not everything is new however, large parts of the medieval fabric of the South Gate and North Gate survived and have been restored, and the huge Guest Hall has also been renovated and now serves as an exhibition area.

There's an audio-visual presentation, an exhibition, tea

THE BUCKFAST BEE
Among apiarists the name Buckfast is world famous, thanks largely to the pioneering work of Brother Adam who has devoted over 70 years to beekeeping at the abbey, including breeding a new kind of bee. The Buckfast Bee is disease resistant, gentle, rarely swarms and of course provides excellent honey. In order to protect their characteristics these are kept well away from other bees at dedicated bee-breeding stations in the centre of Dartmoor.

If the commercial activities at Buckfast seem overwhelming, reflect in peace in the remarkable Abbey Church

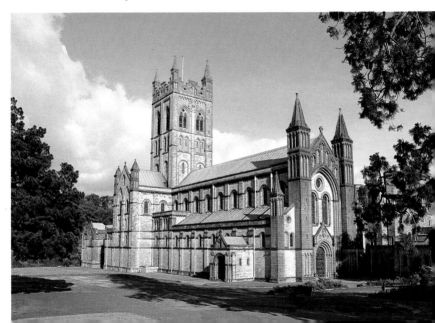

rooms and the Abbey shops where you can stock up on Benedictine honey and the famous Buckfast Tonic Wine. These products are the most obvious way in which the Abbey maintains self-sufficiency but another important source of income is its expertise in stained-glass windows. Over the last 50 years, three of the monks have designed and made windows for over 150 churches as well as many private commissions. Just look at the Abbey's own superb examples – particularly the great east window, the work of Father Charles – and you'll see why they are in such demand.

About the only thing you can't do is go inside the actual monastic quarters, but the exhibitions will satisfy most of your curiosity and there's always a friendly monk on hand to answer questions.

The exploits of Buckland Abbey's most famous owner, navigator and naval hero Sir Francis Drake, are recalled in exhibitions in the house

DRAKE'S DRUM
The most famous piece of Drake memorabilia at Buckland Abbey is Drake's Drum, rescued by his brother Thomas, when the great man died of dysentery on the Spanish Main in 1596. Tradition has it that should England, in dire need, ever need the services of Drake again the drum will beat of its own accord. Other Drake relics include contemporary paintings, ship models, personal firearms, flags and medals.

BUCKLAND ABBEY Map ref SX4867

Don't come to Buckland Abbey harbouring visions of hooded figures and Gregorian Chant. If the Cistercians, who were evicted from here in 1539, came back tomorrow they would scarcely recognise the place. Following the Dissolution, the Abbey was sold to Richard Grenville, a cousin to Walter Raleigh and the first in a line of illustrious seafarers to live here. His son Roger Grenville ended up in a watery grave aboard his famous command the *Mary Rose*, and his heir, another Richard Grenville, also met an untimely death, aboard the *Revenge* in 1591. By 1576, however, he had changed the face of the abbey completely, demolishing many of the old monastic buildings including the cloisters, building a Great Hall, and effectively converting it into a rather splendid Elizabethan mansion.

Francis Drake moved into Buckland Abbey in 1582 and stayed for 13 years and it is this connection for which it is best known. The house remained in the direct Drake family line until 1794. The last occupant of Drake descendancy died in 1937 and, following severe fire damage in 1938, the property passed into the care of the National Trust.

A stone corbel here, some delicate tracery there, are the only obvious visible remains of the old abbey and restoration following the fire has not been totally sympathetic. Nonetheless this is still an interesting house to explore, with many fine rooms, including the Great Hall with its ornate plasterwork, a chapel containing several relics of the abbey's fabric and a 16th-century kitchen. Don't miss taking a leisurely stroll around the beautiful grounds and also popping into the craft workshops.

BUCKLAND IN THE MOOR   Map ref SX7273

You may not realise it but you have probably already seen a little bit of Buckland in the Moor. Its thatched cottages, the quintessential English rural retreat, have starred on countless calendars, a thousand 1,000-piece jigsaws, and biscuit tins by the score. The other famous village building is the church; not because it is an outstanding example of Early English architecture (parts of it date back to the 12th century), nor because of its Norman font. Most visitors don't even see its superb screen. The big attraction is its clock face, on which the numerals have been replaced by the twelve letters M Y D E A R M O T H E R – a superlative example of English sentimentality in a perfect setting.

Just east of the village towards Ashburton is a round building, now home to the acclaimed Roundhouse Craft Centre. During the last century this used to hold a horse and gin for grinding corn.

THE GREAT BARN
The architectural highlight of the Buckland Abbey estate, and the only building to survive intact from the Cistercian period, is the 14th-century Great Barn, used by the monks for storage of crops, wool and hides. It has a superb arch-braced roof, measures 159 feet (48m) long by 32 feet (10m) wide and, to the ridge, 60 feet (18m) high, thus making it one of the country's largest barns.

BUCKLAND'S TEN COMMANDMENTS
Just east of Buckland in the Moor is Buckland Beacon, Devon's answer to Mount Sinai, where you will find a version of the the Ten Commandments carved in 1928, on a granite block, to celebrate Parliament's rejection of the proposed new book of Common Prayer.

Picturesque cottages nestle amid the trees in Buckland in the Moor

WILDLIFE ON THE MOORS

With wild open moorland, conifer woods and steep-sided combes of sheltered pastures, there is a wide variety of animal life to be seen on Dartmoor. The woods are home to birds such as crossbills, siskins and redpolls, while on the open moors, especially in the spring, you can see meadow pipits, merlins and ring ouzels. Buzzards are a common sight, and skylarks frequent the wilder areas. Larger animals are mostly of the domestic variety, cows, sheep and Dartmoor ponies, but there are fallow, roe and sika deer.

The river slows down through rocky shallows at Dartmeet

CANONTEIGN FALLS   Map ref SX8383

Canonteign Falls is a privately owned beauty spot comprising lakes and waterfalls including the Lady Exmouth Falls, which, with a sheer drop of 220 feet (67m), is the highest in England. Take the one-mile (1.6km) nature trail through the woodland and you will find lakes and two more falls. This beautiful gorge scenery is partly natural and partly man-made, first landscaped by the aforementioned Lady Exmouth in the late 18th century. The view from the top of Lady Exmouth's Falls is spectacular. Below, waterfowl swim on the lake and pond and a 6-acre wetland nature reserve is stocked with more birds and waterplants. There is a shop and café, an undercover barbecue area and play barn and a large picnic area.

DARTMEET   Map ref SX6773

Dartmoor's two principal rivers are the East Dart and the West Dart. Dartmeet, not surprisingly, is where they come together and is a popular beauty spot with a characteristic Dartmoor clapper bridge (see Postbridge page 70) spanning the river. Like many such places in the area it can get very busy in the high season but a short walk – north along the river is a good bet – will soon take you through the valley where you can enjoy spectacular scenery away from the crowds.

DREWSTEIGNTON   Map ref SX7391

The heart of Drewsteignton is a picture-postcard square with cob and thatch cottages, church and the Drewe Arms pub. The latter is well worth a look inside, even if you are teetotal, for here is that great rarity, a truly unspoilt village pub – there is not even a bar or serving counter. From the square it's a short journey downhill to the 500-year old Fingle Bridge and the start of the glorious Teign Gorge. Spring is a wonderful time with carpets of daffodils and bluebells, and ornithologists will have a field day here. The walk ends after 6½ miles (10.4km) at Steps Bridge, which like Fingle Bridge is an ever-popular and very busy beauty spot.

The other major attraction here is Castle Drogo, which, despite its Gothic name, is less than 75 years old and is in fact the last 'castle' to be built in England (by the foremost English architect of his day, Edwin Lutyens). Its exterior resembles a rather forbidding grey granite fortified country house – some critics have even likened it to a prison – but the interior is far from spartan. The bare granite contrasts beautifully with rich tapestries, Spanish treasure chests and classic Oriental, French and English furnishings in an ingenious marriage of stately home and medieval fortress. There are also several charming Edwardian Arts and Crafts touches, and the bathroom, kitchen, scullery and other 'downstairs' rooms are particular visitor favourites. The grounds enjoy marvellous views over the Teign valley.

Colourful borders contrast with blocks of more formal hedging in the gardens of Castle Drogo

THE DROGO NAME
The Drogo in Castle Drogo comes from an ancient noble Norman ancestor of Julius Drewe, the grocery magnate responsible for the castle's creation. Julius Drewe lived here only briefly and Castle Drogo is now a National Trust property, though the Drewe family still occupy the private rooms of the house.

Bridford Wood and the Teign Valley

A steady climb through Bridford Wood (NT) and across open farmland, affording fine Teign Valley views on the eastern flanks of Dartmoor. This walk is particularly beautiful in springtime, when the wild daffodils, ransoms (wild garlic) and bluebells are in bloom.

Time: 2½ hours. Distance: 3 or 4 miles (4.8 or 6.4km).
Location: 3 miles (4.8km) northeast of Moretonhampstead.
Start: Steps Bridge car park, 1¼ miles (2km) southwest of Dunsford.
(OS grid ref: SX801883.)
OS Map: Explorer 110 (Torquay & Dawlish) 1:25,000.
See Key to Walks on page 121.

ROUTE DIRECTIONS

Cross the road just below the car park opposite Steps Bridge Inn to enter **Bridford Wood** (NT). At the second footpath fingerpost take the bridleway waymarked 'Burnicombe for Bridford' (blue dot), then cross a footbridge over a stream and begin the steady climb up the valley side. Recross the stream (no bridge), turn immediately right with waymarker, disregarding NT permissive path, and continue uphill parallel with the stream.

Pass a NT sign, then a path to your left and proceed to a gate on the woodland fringe. Head across pasture, signposted 'Burnicombe Farm', soon to bear right with a fingerpost across a stream. Turn left up to a gate at the top of the field on to a hedged trackway leading into Burnicombe farmyard.

Keep the farmhouse to your left and climb to a gate ahead with a waymarker post. Pass through, turn left along the field edge to a small gate in the corner. Go straight ahead over the next field to a waymarked stile and on down across the next field to a metal gate by a large holly tree into a hedged trackway.

Gently descend. Near the private gate to Lowton Farm, turn sharp left through a metal gate into a field and keep right-handed along the field edge to an arrowed gate by a barn. Turn left, then almost immediately right through a gate and proceed downhill on an old sunken green lane, through four

River levels permitting, why not make the detour to the pretty village of Dunsford

333

3333

gates and eventually reach a narrow metalled lane.

Bear left (ignore signed path left), follow the almost traffic-free lane downhill. Eventually pass the driveway to 'Shooting Box' house and turn left on an arrowed grass-centred track for 'Steps Bridge' (private road, public path). Enter Bridford Wood by NT sign, keep to track above the **River Teign** to a junction of paths and a fingerpost.

To visit **Dunsford** village (refreshments at Royal Oak), turn right and follow the waymarked path across the stepping stones in the river (take care), cross the road and turn right for a short distance, then left through a gate signed 'Dunsford Village' and follow the yellow waymarks across three fields into a lane leading to the village. Turn right for the inn. Retrace your steps back to the fingerpost in Bridford Wood. *Note:* after periods of prolonged rain the stepping stones may be impassable.

Continue through the woodland, following the main path left around the perimeter fence of a house and garden. Continue to **Steps Bridge**.

POINTS OF INTEREST

Bridford Wood
Until the beginning of the 20th century much of this area of mixed deciduous woodland was coppiced every 25 years for making charcoal, fencing posts and tan bark. Level platforms, where the charcoal burners built fires, can be seen among the trees.

Covering the steep valley slopes above the Teign, the woodland is famous for its wild flowers, including snowdrops, daffodils, wood anemones and bluebells. There is a wide variety of wildlife here, notably buzzards, wood warblers, fallow deer and badgers.

River Teign
The Teign rises high up on Dartmoor, flowing through steep wooded valleys and pastoral Devon countryside on its way to the sea at Teignmouth. At Steps Bridge the clear fast-flowing waters hold trout and salmon, while along the riverbanks are kingfishers, herons and the predatory mink. Otters have occasionally been seen.

Dunsford
This charming village of whitewashed cob and thatch cottages has a winding street climbing to 15th-century St Mary's Church. In the churchyard is St Thomas's cross, part of an octagonal preaching cross which once stood at the top of the hill on the eastern approach to the village. Two miles (3.2km) northwest of the village is Great Fulford, seat of the Fulford family since at least the 12th century, though the present building is mainly Tudor.

Steps Bridge
A plaque on the bridge states that the present bridge was constructed in 1816, and the carved names of Bridford and Dunsford denote that the river forms the boundary between the two parishes.

The inn at Holne was ideally set to catch passing carriage trade on its way over the moor to Buckfastleigh

CYCLING ON DARTMOOR
Cycling in Devon, particularly on Dartmoor, is a challenging prospect requiring a good level of fitness and a well-geared bicycle to cope with the steeply undulating terrain. Gentler cycling country can be found on the sheltered southeastern edge of Dartmoor, where an intricate web of narrow rolling lanes explores the beautiful Dart Valley. Opportunities abound for all cyclists of varying levels of ability. Short family rides can incorporate the delights of the River Dart Country Park and Buckfast Abbey, while a leisurely day's tour can link the picturesque villages of Holne, Buckland in the Moor and Widecombe in the Moor. Well-equipped off-road cycling enthusiasts can escape the crowds by venturing up on to the open moor by the many tracks and bridleways that criss-cross the area.

THE TWO MOORS WAY
This long distance footpath links Exmoor, just south of Lynton, and the southern edge of Dartmoor at Ivybridge.

HOLNE Map ref SX7969
This pretty village 3 miles (4.8km) north of Buckfastleigh stands on the edge of Dartmoor. It is famous as being the home of Charles Kingsley (author of *The Water Babies*, *Westward Ho!* and *Hereward the Wake*) who was born at the Rectory in 1819. It's a quiet place, which doesn't attract too many visitors and there are two charming refreshment options. The village pub, the 14th-century Church House Inn, which takes its name from the days when it (like many other Church House Inns in Devon) brewed beer for the Church on feast days and enjoyed a close association with the clergy.

IVYBRIDGE Map ref SX6356
This small, often overlooked town on the River Erme probably owes its name to the picturesque 13th-century humpbacked bridge which still spans the river today. There's nothing of great interest in the town itself but a walk north along the river is recommended. At Longtimbers Wood (just a few minutes away) you will see some impressive granite pillars – all that remains of the viaduct that Brunel built in 1848 for the Great Western Railway which once ran through here.

Just northwest of Ivybridge at Sparkwell is the popular Dartmoor Wildlife Park and Falconry Centre. This is an entertaining zoo park, set in beautifully landscaped countryside and features birds of prey, lions, tigers, seals, bison and bears among its collection of around 150 species.

LUSTLEIGH Map ref SX7881
The focal point of this charming village is the 13th-century Church of St John, with a fine screen and some interesting memorials which recall 14th-century knights. Clustered around the centre of the village are a number of handsome old thatched buildings of late medieval origin, including the idyllic sunny-yellow Primrose Cottage tea rooms and the whitewashed 15th-century Cleave Inn. Just one mile (1.6km) to the west of the

Lustleigh's 13th-century church provides the central focus of this pretty village,

village is the well-known beauty spot of Lustleigh Cleave, a moorland valley where the River Bovey flows through an avenue of trees.

LYDFORD   Map ref SX5185

This lovely unspoilt village is famous for its gorge and its castle, a plain, small, square ruined keep, built in 1195, which in medieval times gained notoriety as a prison court where it was customary to hang and draw first and ask questions later. The focus of the village is around the 16th-century oak-timbered Castle Inn, which was once the rector's home and contains a collection of 1,000-year old pennies minted at Lydford during the reign of Ethelred II. Next door is the Church of St Petrock, largely 15th century and in early medieval times the largest parish in England – anyone dying within its 50,000-acre area of jurisdiction had to be buried here. Not surprisingly St Petrock is famous for its graveyard where there are numerous interesting tombstones.

Just outside the village is the wooded valley of Lydford Gorge (National Trust) which stretches for 1½ miles (2.4km) and in places is up to 60 feet (18m) deep. A spectacular riverside walk ends at the 90-feet (27m) high White Lady waterfall; en route the river has scooped a series of potholes where the water bubbles and boils, most notably in the thundering Devil's Cauldron.

A TIMELESS MEMORIAL
The most amusing gravestone epitaph in St Petrock's Churchyard is as follows:
    'Here lies in horizontal position the outside case of George Routleigh (died 1802) watchmaker, Wound up, In hope of being taken in hand, By his Maker, And of being thoroughlye cleaned repaired, And set agoing, In the World to come'

A costumed guide takes on the role of a kitchen maid in the 'living history' presentation at Morwellham Quay

NINE MAIDENS DANCING
Dartmoor is littered with standing stones, stone circles, stone rows and stone tombs. Many of these prehistoric remains are little understood even today and attract bizarre legends. One of the best known formations is The Nine Maidens on Belstone Common just south of Okehampton. According to one version of the legend these standing stones, which actually number 16 or 17 according to your definition, come to life and dance on the Hunter's Moon (the first moon after the full moon nearest to the autumn equinox). Another version has it that they dance every day at noon. It's not so difficult to check the latter, just turn up at 12 o'clock and watch!

MORWELLHAM QUAY Map ref SX4570

It's difficult to imagine today but between 1844 and 1859 this tranquil rural idyll deep in the Tamar Valley, was the Klondike of its day, gripped by 'copper fever' when great deposits of copper ore were discovered locally. Morwellham Quay was the furthest navigable point on the River Tamar and several quays, a dock big enough to take six 300-ton schooners and a 4½-mile (7.2km) railway line were hurriedly built, followed by cottages to house the 200-strong community of miners, assayers and blacksmiths. But as the five mines were exhausted and river transport was superseded by the railways, boom turned to bust. By 1880, after some 700,000 tons of copper and 70,000 tons of arsenic had been extracted from the Tamar Valley, it was all over and the riverside port returned to its natural slumbers.

Morwellham Quay lay forgotten until 1970 when the Dartington Trust stepped in to restore it to its former glory. Today the quays and buildings are alive again with visitors exploring the fascinating infrastructure and chatting to local 'workers' (costumed actor-guides) who are faithful to their mid 19th-century time warp down to the very last detail. The highlight of the visit is a trip deep into an actual copper mine aboard an electric tramway, but there is lots more: horse-drawn carriage rides, a ship to explore, costumes to try on, demonstrations by blacksmiths and assayers and a farm to wander around – allow a whole day.

OKEHAMPTON Map ref SX5995

Okehampton is the main town of north Dartmoor, boasting a range of shops for locals as well as tourists, including a quaint Victorian covered arcade. Its high street (Fore Street) is dominated by the 14th-century tower of the Chapel of St James. At the opposite end of this street, tucked away in a charming cobbled courtyard (adjacent to the White Hart Inn) are craft studios, tearooms and the excellent Museum of Dartmoor Life. This is housed in an early 19th-century mill complete with working waterwheel and is bristling with many weird and wonderful old objects relating to Dartmoor crafts and industries. A famous 'Dartmoor letterbox' can also be found here (see page 50).

A short walk from the centre are the ruins of Okehampton Castle (English Heritage). Parts date back to Norman times, though most of what remains today was built in the early 14th century by the Courtenay (Earls of Devon) family. Following the execution of the Earl in 1538 the castle was destroyed by Henry VIII. Today just enough remains to give a good idea of what it looked like without overtaxing the imagination. An entertaining personal stereo tour guides visitors around the various buildings, at the same time bringing to life a supposed day in the life of the lady of the castle in medieval times. The setting, high on a hill overlooking the river and the beautiful woodlands which were once used as a royal deer park, is majestic.

THE GHOST OF LADY HOWARD

Lady Mary Howard of Okehampton Castle has been described as a wicked woman who married for money then murdered her husbands, and also as a victim of a marital system in which orphaned heiresses had little say in whom they married. Certainly she was married four times, first at the age of 12, and she outlived every one of her husbands. But whatever the circumstances, her life was not an easy one. Even in death she is said not to get any rest, condemned to travel nightly between Tavistock and Okehampton Castle in a coach made of human bones, preceded by a huge black dog with flaming eyes.

The surprisingly substantial remains of Okehampton Castle

Dartmoor and the Tamar Valley

This 62-mile (100-km) drive skirts the northwestern edge of Dartmoor before climbing on to its most spectacular, granite-dotted open moorland. From the most southerly point of the drive, the return is through the beautiful countryside of the Tamar Valley. The drive begins in Okehampton, which has an attractive wide main street, flanked by some fine old buildings. Just off the main street is a cobbled courtyard housing a variety of craft workshops and the Museum of Dartmoor Life. Overlooking the town and the surrounding countryside are the impressive ruins of Okehampton Castle.

ROUTE DIRECTIONS

See Key to Car Tours on page 120.
From the town centre take the B3260, signposted 'Tavistock'. In 3 miles (4.8km) cross a road bridge and turn right on to the A30, signposted 'Launceston'. In a mile (1.6km) take the A386, signed 'Tavistock' and 'Plymouth' and continue for 9 miles (14.5km) to Mary Tavy, a peaceful village now, but once home of the largest copper mine in the world. Remains of mine workings are dotted around the hillsides. Continue for 3¾ miles (6km), with fine views of Dartmoor on the left, to Tavistock. One of four stannary towns around the moor, Tavistock, though much older, is essentially a product of 19th-century prosperity. It has a thriving covered market and bustling main street and is one of the most attractive 'working' towns in the county.

Just before reaching the town centre, turn left on to the B3357, signposted 'Princetown'. The road soon climbs on to open moorland with huge outcrops of granite all around, including Cox Tor and Great Mis Tor on the left.

In 6½ miles (10.5km) turn right, signed 'Princetown', and continue for a mile (1.6km) to Princetown, with sombre views down over the prison to the left. Pass the Dartmoor Prison Museum and the excellent High Moorland Visitor Centre, then turn right at a roundabout on to the B3212 signed 'Yelverton, Plymouth', a road which has some of the most spectacular views on the moor. In 6¼

Looking from Yelverton across to Sheepstor church and the blue waters of Burrator Reservoir

miles (10.1km) reach a round-about and take the first exit on to the A386, signposted 'Plymouth'.

In 300 yards (275m) turn right, signposted 'Crapstone, Buckland Monachorum, Milton Combe', with brown tourist signs to The Garden House and Buckland Abbey. In 1¼ miles (2km) detour left to visit **Buckland Abbey**, a splendid former monastic foundation which was later the home of Sir Francis Drake. On the main route continue, passing **The Garden House** in half a mile (0.8km) on the right. In another half mile (0.8km) turn left, signposted 'Milton Combe' and 'Bere Alston'. In another half mile (0.8km) turn right, signposted 'Bere Alston', descending through a delightful wooded valley to cross the River Tavy at a picturesque stone bridge, following signs for 'Bere Alston'. Ascend a 1-in-4 (25%) hill and in 2 miles (3.2km) turn right, signed 'Gulworthy' and 'Tavistock'. In another 2½ miles (4km) detour left for a mile (1.6km) to visit **Morwellham Quay.** This once thriving copper mine and port has been accurately renovated and restored to form a splendid open-air museum, staffed by craftsmen and other workers in period costume.

On the main route continue for 1½ miles (2.4km) to meet the A390. Cross the main road and continue forward, signed 'Chipshop', 'Lamerton' and 'Milton Abbot'. In 4¾ miles (7.8km) cross the B3362, then in 1¼ miles (2km) turn right, signposted 'Brentor'. In a further mile (1.6km) at crossroads, go straight on, signed 'Brentor'. In 1½ miles (2.4km) reach the car park for **Brent Tor Church** on the right. Perched atop a high grassy mound

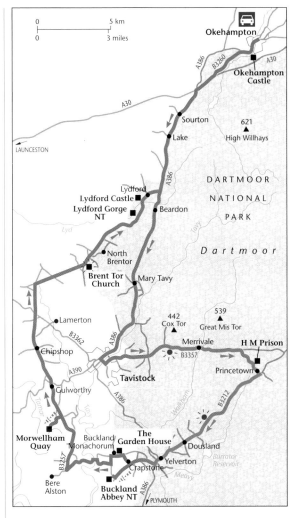

with great rocks strewn all around, the church enjoys panoramic views on all sides.

Shortly after the car park turn left, signed 'Brentor' and 'Lydford'.

In 3 miles (4.8km) pass the first entrance to **Lydford Gorge** on the left. This beautiful wooded gorge, owned by the National Trust, has a 3½-mile (5.6-km) walk with a waterfall at one end and the spectacular Devil's Cauldron at the other. Continue for

1½ miles (2.4km) to reach Lydford Castle, a great square stone keep which dates from 1195.

In three quarters of a mile (1.2km) turn left on to the A386, signposted 'Okehampton'. In 5¾ miles (9.2km) turn right on to the A30, signed 'Okehampton' and 'Exeter'. In a mile (1.6km) turn left, signed 'Okehampton' and follow the B3260 for 3 miles (4.8km) back to the town centre.

THE PILGRIM FATHERS
The most famous Barbican landmark is the Island House, a late 16th-century building on Southside Street where the Pilgrim Fathers supposedly spent their last night in England. A plaque on the wall lists all 102 names. A few yards away are the Mayflower Steps, the point at which they actually embarked for the New World. A plethora of plaques marks this and many other famous expeditions.

PLYMOUTH   Map ref SX4754

Plymouth's seafaring legacy is legendary. Naturally blessed with one of Europe's finest deepwater anchorages, the patronage of Sir Francis Drake and Sir John Hawkins established the port's supremacy in the 16th century. And it was, of course, from here in 1588 that Drake sailed to crush the Armada, though he did have time to finish his game of bowls first, or so the story goes. In 1620 a more peaceable crew, the Pilgrim Fathers, set off from Plymouth aboard the *Mayflower* to make a new life in North America and to lay the foundation for New England. In later years Captain Cooke launched his voyages of discovery from here and in the 19th century both colonists and convicts set sail to Australia from Plymouth. Recent history has not been so kind – the city was devastated during World War II and the centre has been completely rebuilt, but much of the old harbour area survived.

Start your visit on the grassy Hoe (it means high place or hill) for a marvellous view over Plymouth Sound and its busy shipping lanes. Smeaton's Tower, the archetypal red-and-white lighthouse in the middle of the Hoe, was built in 1759 and once stood on the treacherous Eddystone Rocks, 14 miles (22km) out to sea. It was replaced in 1882 by a bigger lighthouse and reassembled here. Climb to the top for panoramic views. Just below the lighthouse is The Dome, which through high-tech audio-visual displays and hands-on exhibits provides an informative and entertaining interpretation of Plymouth's history. You can even scan the shipping on the Sound, using cameras, radar and satellite technology.

Next to the Hoe is the Royal Citadel, a powerful star-shaped fortress built 1666–75. It is now home to a commando regiment but guided tours in summer

Smeaton's Tower, formerly the Eddystone lighthouse, looks across to Drake's Island, once used as a prison

Plymouth's attractive old heart is the Barbican, with delightful corners to explore around the harbour

(tickets from the Dome) show the most interesting buildings, including the Royal Chapel of St Katherine (rebuilt in 1845). Just below the Citadel is the National Marine Aquarium, with displays in vast tanks.

Keep walking down the hill and you will reach the Barbican, Plymouth's old harbour area. Several pleasure trips set off from here, the most popular being a one-hour tour around the dockyards. The oldest part of the Barbican is New Street, an historic cobbled street built in 1581, lined with timber-framed and jettied houses, including the atmospheric Elizabethan House, a rare surviving typical Tudor house which once belonged to a sea captain. Also on New Street is a charming small Elizabethan garden. On Barbican Quay you will find the new and exciting Mayflower Centre where you can learn about the history of the Barbican and experience the amazing story of the Pilgrim Fathers and the *Mayflower*.

In the modern centre of town, just a short walk north, some interesting old buildings survived the wartime bombing. On Finewell Street is the Prysten House (also known as Yogges House), a splendid merchant's home and the oldest (1498) dwelling in the city, built around three sides of a galleried courtyard. A few yards away is the Merchant's House, a classic four-storey Elizabethan building now housing a lively museum and a fully-stocked apothecary's shop. The City Museum and Art Gallery holds an outstanding collection of fine and decorative arts and holds some good temporary exhibitions throughout the year.

PLYMOUTH GIN

On Southside Street in the Barbican area you will find the Plymouth Gin distillery, the oldest of its kind in England, which has been here since 1793 – a guided tour shows not only the distilling process, but also the ancient building which contains it. The buildings are the oldest in the city; their exact age and original purpose is disputed but they may have started life in 1425 as a Blackfriars monastery.

Postbridge boasts Dartmoor's finest clapper bridge, spanning the East Dart

A GUNPOWDER FACTORY
One mile (1.6km) southwest of Postbridge on the B3212 is Powder Mills, built in 1844 as a gunpowder factory. Local quarry blasting provided a market until the invention of dynamite in 1867 and the factory closed in the 1890s. Today only its chimneys remain but pottery workshops have been set up in the cottages which were once home to the gunpowder factory workers.

POSTBRIDGE Map ref SX6579
Postbridge is classic Dartmoor. There isn't really a great deal here – a scattering of farms and cottages, a chapel and an inn, but Postbridge is a favourite starting and finishing point for Dartmoor walkers of all ages and abilities. Whether you want to join one of the numerous guided tours that depart from here or simply want information and maps in order to plan your own hike, you'll find helpful advice in the information office.

Postbridge's other claim to fame is its clapper bridge. This type of crossing is unique to Dartmoor and was built by medieval farmers and tin-workers in the 13th or 14th century. There are 30 such bridges on Dartmoor but the one at Postbridge is the best example of all. Its four huge slabs of granite, weighing up to 8 tons each and measuring up to 15 feet (4.5m) long by 7 feet (2m) wide, have been carefully placed over the East Dart on three granite piers, just like rough-hewn building pieces from a baby giant's construction kit. The adjacent road bridge dates from the 1780s.

PRINCETOWN Map ref SX5873
Princetown is Dartmoor at is bleakest, greyest and grimmest. No wonder then that this spot was chosen for Dartmoor prison. It was built in 1806 to house French prisoners captured during the Napoleonic Wars, and in 1812–14 it confined Americans taken during the War of Independence. Conditions were grim and overcrowded

and around 1,000 Frenchmen and Americans died here from gaol fever. From 1816 to 1850 the prison stood empty until it was revived for criminal offenders. The Prison Museum, housed in the old prison stables, unlocks the fascinating history of Dartmoor Prison.

At 1,400 feet (427m) above sea level, Princetown claims to be the highest town in England (though in fact it is little more than a village). However, its altitude makes it the natural centre of the 'High Moorland' and there is a good visitor centre and information point in the restored early 19th-century Old Duchy Hotel.

SALTRAM HOUSE   Map ref SX5155

Saltram House is Plymouth's very own grand country mansion, in fact it is the largest house in Devon. It lies just within the city boundary (unfortunately close to the busy A38), yet its setting, high above the River Plym in 300 acres of beautiful parkland, is completely bucolic. The house is a classic 18th-century mansion, enlarged and remodelled for the Parker family in 1740 from a 16th-century house. It is remarkable for its state of preservation and is also a showcase for the work of Robert Adam and Joshua Reynolds. Adam's magnificent interior plasterwork and decoration is most prominent in the saloon and in the dining room (completed 1768). Reynolds, the most fashionable English portrait artist of his day, was a master at the local grammar school and a personal friend of the Parkers. As a result of this close connection, 14 full-length portraits hang in the house. The artistic tradition lives on in the chapel which houses a gallery of West Country art. The Great Kitchen is another highlight of the house, while the gardens, which include an orangery, are also well worth exploring.

REYNOLDS AT SALTRAM
From 1770 onwards the artist Joshua Reynolds came to Saltram House on a regular basis, becoming firm friends with Lord Boringdon and his family and undertaking more commissions from them than from any other of his regular customers. Saltram still has many of the artist's paintings on display, including a portrait of his patron which is considered unique. During his frequent visits to Saltram, Reynolds liked nothing better than a day's hunting or shooting, unless it was to partake in one of the gambling parties organised by Lord Boringdon, where the size of the stakes were legendary.

Saltram's exquisite saloon is decorated to the designs of Robert Adam

WEST DEVON STICKLEPATH CYCLE ROUTE
This 30-mile (48km) circular route, from Sticklepath skirts the northern fringes of Dartmoor and follows the Rivers Taw and Okement, passing through Hatherleigh and Okehampton. The route takes in pretty villages with village stocks and traditional blacksmiths and passes old manor houses.

The West Devon Sticklepath Cycle Route, the Tarka Trail cycleway (see page 44) and the Mid Torridge Link (see page 41) form a complete cycle route from Dartmoor to the north Devon coast.

STICKLEPATH   Map ref SX6494

Stickle means steep (in Anglo-Saxon) and the steep path in question once ran down from the village to the River Taw. The Taw at this point runs swiftly off the moor and during the Industrial Revolution its energy was harnessed by several waterwheels in Sticklepath to grind corn, to help spin wool and to power a small factory making agricultural hand tools. The latter, now known as the Finch Foundry (National Trust), survived from 1814 right up to 1960. After a brief period of closure it was restored to partial working order and re-opened as a museum of industrial history. Though this may sound pretty dull fare, it's quite a sight when the sluices are opened. The powerful waterwheels start turning and these drive cogs and pulleys in the most delightful Heath Robinson fashion in order to set the ancient machinery in motion. There are three wheels: one either hammers the raw iron 'bloom' to make wrought iron or powers metal-cutting shears; another grinds or polishes metal or cuts wood; the third powers a fan, which acts as a bellows to heat the furnaces and forges. The Foundry isn't just a study in industrial engineering however. Its working practices and its relationship to the small village also make it an interesting study in social history, not to mention alternative energy, and these aspects too are explained to visitors.

One of the restored waterwheels at the Finch Foundry, which once supplied agricultural tools to the local area

TAVISTOCK Map ref SX4874

Tavistock today is little more than a pleasant market town but it was once home to the most powerful abbey in southwest England. Parts of the Benedictine structure still stand, the abbey gateway has been incorporated into the Town Hall and opposite here, its infirmary dining hall is now a chapel. Betsey Grimbal's Tower (the Abbey's west gatehouse) stands next to the Bedford Hotel and part of the cloisters is retained in the yard of the handsome 15th-century Church of St Eustace.

The town's second great period of wealth came in the 13th century with tin mining when Tavistock became the largest of Devon's four Stannary towns. By the time tin was exhausted in the 17th century a thriving cloth trade was prospering in Tavistock and then along came the great 'copper-rush' of the mid to late 19th century when a rich lode was discovered locally. As boom turned to bust Tavistock depopulated from 9,000 to 6,000 inhabitants and readjusted to its original role as market town – today Tavistock's famous Victorian covered Pannier Market (see page 16) is rarely free of stalls, with different goods on different days.

Tavistock's most famous son is Francis Drake, born in 1542 at Crowndale Farm just south of the town. There's nothing to see there, but there is a fine statue at the end of Plymouth Road in the town centre. This is the original (cast in 1883) of the famous one on Plymouth Hoe, which is a copy.

Bedford Square stands on the site of Tavistock's former abbey; a market has been held here since 1105

STANNARY TOWNS

The word 'Stannary' simply means tin, and Stannary Towns were those to which miners on Dartmoor brought their ingots to be weighed, assayed and hopefully given the King's Stamp. The other Stannary Towns were Ashburton, Chagford and Plympton.

Walkham Valley and Buckland Monachorum

A pleasant mix of wooded riverside paths, quiet country lanes and open field and moorland paths. On clear days there are wonderful views across the Tamar Valley into Cornwall and towards the prominent tors on the western side of Dartmoor. The walk can get muddy in places.

Time: 2½ hours. Distance: 4½ miles (7.2km).
Location: 3 miles (4.8km) southeast of Tavistock.
Start: Bedford Bridge car park, on A386 near Horrabridge.
(OS grid ref: SX504703.)
OS Map: Outdoor Leisure 28 (Dartmoor)
1:25,000.
See Key to Walks on page 121.

ROUTE DIRECTIONS

From the far end of the parking area cross a small footbridge on a path into the woods. Where the path divides, keep right along the left bank of the river through **Walkham Valley** (path may be indistinct). In a mile (1.6km), at a track near a parking area, turn right to view **Grenofen Bridge**, which spans the river. Retrace your steps along this old track and ascend steeply, zig-zagging through Sticklepath Wood. The stony green lane eventually levels out on to Roborough Down, becoming grassy as it crosses scrubland, with fine views across the Tavy Valley, and back towards the rugged mass of Dartmoor.

Keep ahead, ignoring side paths, pass a parking area on the left, go through a gate beside a cattle grid and follow the now metalled lane past Bymoor House and Downlane Farm. Go ahead at a crossroads and keep on this quiet lane for half a mile (0.8km) to **Buckland Monachorum**. At a T-junction turn left, signed 'Crapstone', and bear right at a small roundabout to follow the village lane past the school to the church.

Take the waymarked footpath left around the side of the church, pass through a kissing gate and climb an unusual stone stile. Keep left through a second kissing gate, cross a field to a stile, go over the stile and follow the right-hand field edge to a stile near a barn. Bear left over a stile to a track (can be muddy), cross a stone stile and follow the hedged trackway, shortly to reach a gate and lane.

Turn right along the lane, gradually climbing up to a cattle grid and junction of

Stone cottages line the quiet streets of Buckland Monachorum

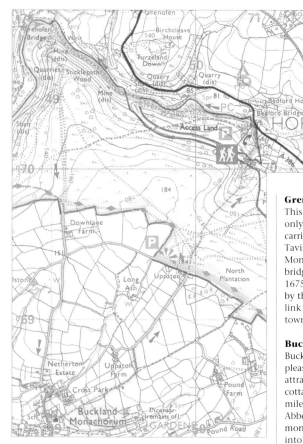

lanes beside Uppaton Lodge. Cross straight over on to **Roborough Down** on a wide grassy swath through heathland. After 50 yards (46m), bear off right and pass though a small stone-lined nick in a low grassy bank. Keep straight ahead towards a mast and houses, heading downhill on a grassy path and in 100 yards (92m) bear left on an initially narrower path and continue, ignoring all cross paths, to the valley.

Pass beneath the impressive Magpie viaduct, keeping right, by the fence, to a wall. Turn left down a defined trackway that leads back into Bedford Bridge car park.

POINTS OF INTEREST

Walkham Valley

The remains of the railway and industrial workings litter this attractive wooded river valley. The Plymouth to Tavistock railway line passed through the Walkham Valley, and the Walkham Viaduct (367 yards/336m long and 132 feet/40m high) crossed the valley between Bedford Bridge and Grenofen Bridge.

The railway line was closed in 1962, after operating for 102 years and the viaduct was later blown up, but odd chunks of masonry can still be seen above the surface.

Grenofen Bridge

This tiny single-arch bridge, only 7 feet (2m) wide, once carried the main route from Tavistock to Buckland Monachorum. A previous bridge existed well before 1675 and was probably built by the Church for monks to link the abbeys in the two towns.

Buckland Monachorum

Buckland 'of the monks' is a pleasant village with some attractive 17th-century cottages. It lies less than a mile (1.6km) from Buckland Abbey, built by Cistercian monks in 1278. Converted into a mansion in 1541 by Sir Richard Grenville, it was later bought by Sir Francis Drake in 1581. Now owned by the National Trust, it houses a Drake Museum and is full of relics associated with the great sailor. One prized exhibit is Drake's Drum, rescued by his brother Thomas who was with the great sailor when he died of dysentery on the Spanish Main in 1596.

Roborough Down

This area of open heathland is located just within the Dartmoor National Park and has a magnificent view of Dartmoor. On clear days Brent Tor church and many prominent tors can be seen.

Four people died and many were injured in Widecombe in 1638, when a lightning bolt knocked one of the pinnacles down from the tower into the church below

THE FAMOUS FOLK SONG
No-one is quite sure when Widecombe (or Widdicombe) Fair actually started or when people first started singing about it, but the words of the famous folk song were published in 1880 by the vicar of another parish who heard them sung by an old countryman. It was said that to be able to remember the chorus 'wi' Bill Brewer, Jan Stewer, Peter Gurney, Peter Davey, Dan'l Whiddon, Harry Hawk, Old Uncle Tom Cobley and all' was proof of sobriety. If Bill Brewer and company did exist, they probably came from Spreyton, 12 miles (19.2km) to the north.

WIDECOMBE IN THE MOOR Map ref SX7176
This picturesque Dartmoor village, set in rolling green hills, surrounded by high granite-strewn ridges, really does attract Uncle Tom Cobley and all in summer and at peak times its charm is somewhat overwhelmed. However, despite the tea rooms and tourist paraphernalia, little has changed here over the centuries. The famous Fair is still celebrated on the second Tuesday in September, but its remit has grown from the simple horse-trading fair it once was to accommodate the coachloads who now descend upon it.

The spire of the village Church of St Pancras, 'the Cathedral of the Moors', is a landmark for many miles. The church was built in the 14th century and enlarged in the following two centuries, partly paid for by Dartmoor's tin miners. It is a large building, stretching over 100 feet (30.5m), and its most notable feature is its fine roof bosses. Look out for the sign of the three rabbits. Ironically this gentle docile emblem, linked to alchemy, was adopted by the tin miners (the sign of three hares was also used by them). A less docile crowd you could never wish to meet; Sir Walter Raleigh, in his capacity as Warden of the Stannaries (tin mines), once described them as 'the roughest and most mutinous men in England'.

The adjacent Church House (National Trust) dates back to 1537 when it was a brewhouse, producing Church Ales (see Holne on page 62). It also acted as a rest house for outlying farming families who had a very long distance to travel to Widecombe to attend services. It later became almshouses, then a school and nowadays it serves as the local village hall. The adjacent Sexton's Cottage is now a National Trust and Dartmoor information centre and shop.

If you want to drink in the real atmosphere of Widecombe the pleasant main village pub, the Old Inn, dates back to the 14th century, but it has been much altered and is often packed with visitors. Walk a little way past and you'll find the ancient Rugglestone Inn, one of the least altered pubs in England. There's not even a bar counter, just a half-door where you are served from the tap-room.

YELVERTON Map ref SX5267

The actual village of Yelverton is of little interest, though it is home to unusual attractions, such as the Yelverton Paperweight Centre which displays over 800 of these curious heavy glass blobs, both antique and modern. One mile (1.6km) east of Yelverton is the delightful, little-visited village of Meavy with a whitewashed pub, a medieval church and a manor house that once belonged to the Drake family.

A little further to the east the rocky crag of Sheepstor crowns the skyline. A tiny, pretty hamlet clusters together and looks down over the Burrator Reservoir. Water from here supplies Plymouth and it is said that the very first leat (waterway) to provide the city with drinking water was cut in 1590 by Sir Francis Drake during the time when he was mayor of the city.

A little to the west of Yelverton, at Buckland Monachorum, is the Garden House with a delightful walled garden with an enormous range of colourful plants. The house is also open during summer to garden visitors for lunch and afternoon tea.

THE DANCING TREE
On the village green in Meavy, east of Yelverton, stands an oak tree which is said to be 800 years old – now supported by metal props and the churchyard wall. It is said that nine men once dined in here, and in ancient times it was a 'dancing tree' where pagan rites and dances were performed.

Beside the ancient oak at Meavy, near Yelverton, stands a pub named in its honour

Dartmoor and the Tamar Valley

Leisure Information
Places of Interest
Shopping
The Performing Arts
Sports, Activities and the Outdoors
Annual Events and Customs

Checklist

Leisure Information

TOURIST INFORMATION CENTRES

Ivybridge
South Dartmoor TIC, Leonards Road. Tel: 01752 897035.
Okehampton
Museum Courtyard, 3 West Street. Tel: 01837 53020 (seasonal).
Plymouth
Island House, 9 The Barbican. Tel: 01752 304849.
Tavistock
Town Hall, Bedford Square. Tel: 01822 612938.

DARTMOOR NATIONAL PARK CENTRES

Dartmoor National Park Authority Headquarters
Parke, Haytor Road, Bovey Tracey. Tel: 01626 832093.
Haytor
The Car Park. Tel: 01364 661520.
Newbridge
Riverside Car Park. Tel: 01364 631303.
Postbridge
The Car Park. Tel: 01822 880272.
Princetown
The High Moorland Visitor Centre, Tavistock Road. Tel: 01822 890414.

OTHER INFORMATION

Devon Wildlife Trust
Shirehampton House, 35–37 St David's Hill, Exeter. Tel: 01392 279244.
English Heritage
29 Queen Square, Bristol. Tel: 0117 975 0700
www.english-heritage.org.uk
Forest Enterprise England
340 Bristol Business Park, Coldharbour Lane, Bristol. Tel: 0117 906 6000.
National Trust for Devon
Killerton House, Broadclyst, Exeter. Tel: 01392 881691.
www.nationaltrust.org.uk
English Nature Devonteam
Level 2 Renslade House, Bonhay Road, Exeter. Tel: 01392 88970.
Parking: Plymouth
Park-and-ride schemes operate from Central Park and Marsh Mills to the city centre.
South West Lakes Trust
Highercombe Park, Lewdown, Okehampton. Tel: 01837 871565.

ORDNANCE SURVEY MAPS

Explorer 1:25,000. Sheet 28
Landranger 1:50,000. Sheets 191, 201, 202.

Places of Interest

Unless otherwise stated, there will be an admission charge to the following places of interest.
Becka Falls
Manaton, near Bovey Tracey. Tel: 01647 221259. Open mid-Mar to Oct, daily; winter weekends, Christmas school hols and Feb half term.
Buckfast Abbey
Buckfastleigh. Tel: 01364 645500. Open all year, daily.
Buckfast Butterflies and Dartmoor Otter Sanctuary
Buckfastleigh. Tel: 01364 642916. Open Mar–Oct, daily.
Buckland Abbey
Buckland Monachorum. Tel: 01822 853607. Open end Mar–early Nov, most days. Winter weekends only.
Canonteign Falls
3 miles/4.8km off A38. Tel: 01647 252434. Open early Mar–Oct most days, limited opening in winter.
Castle Drogo
Drewsteignton. Tel: 01647 433306. Open Mar–early Nov most days.
City Museum and Art Gallery
Drake Circus, Plymouth. Tel: 01752 304774. Open all year, most days.
Dartmoor Prison Museum
Princetown. Tel: 01822 890305. Open all year, Tue–Sat.

Dartmoor Wildlife Park and Falconry Centre
Sparkwell. Tel: 01752 837209.
Open all year, daily.
Devon Guild of Craftsmen
Riverside Mill, Bovey Tracey.
Tel: 01626 832223. Open all
year daily, except Christmas and
New Year's Day.
Finch Foundry
Sticklepath. Tel: 01837 840046.
Open Apr–early Nov, most days.
The Garden House
Buckland Monachorum,
Yelverton. Tel: 01822 854769.
Open Mar–Oct,daily.
Lydford Gorge
Lydford (off A386). Tel: 01822
820441/820320. Open Apr–Oct
daily; Nov–Mar waterfall
entrance only.
Mayflower Centre
Barbican Quay, Plymouth. Tel:
01752 266030/304849.
Merchant's House Museum
33 St Andrews Street, Plymouth.
Tel: 01752 304774. Open
Easter–Sep most days.
Morwellham Quay
Morwellham. Tel: 01822
832766/833808. Open all year
daily.
Museum of Dartmoor Life
Museum Courtyard, West Street,
Okehampton. Tel: 01837
52295. Open all year, most
days. Closed Christmas and New
Year.
National Marine Aquarium
The Barbican, Plymouth. Tel:
01752 220084. Open all year
daily, except 25 Dec.
Okehampton Castle
Okehampton. Tel: 01837
52844. Open Apr–Oct daily.
Plymouth Dome
The Hoe, Plymouth. Tel: 01752
600608/603300. Open early Apr
to mid-Oct, daily.
Plymouth Gin Distillery
60 Southside Street, Barbican,
Plymouth. Tel 01752 665292.
Guided tours. Open Easter to
Dec.
Prysten House
Catherine Street, Plymouth. Tel:
01752 661414. Open all year,
Mon–Sat.
Roundhouse Craft Centre
Buckland in the Moor,
Ashburton. Tel: 01364 653234.
Open all year.

Royal Citadel
The Hoe, Plymouth. Tel: 01752
775841. Open guided tours
May–Sep.
Saltram House
Plympton. Tel: 01752 333500.
Open Apr–early Nov most days.
Smeatons Tower
The Hoe, Plymouth.
Tel: 01752 600608. Open all
year, daily.
South Devon Valley Railway
The South Devon Railway Trust,
The Station, Buckfastleigh. Tel:
01364 642338. Open Apr–early
Oct.
**Teign Valley Glass and
House of Marbles**
The Old Pottery, Pottery Road,
Bovey Tracey. Tel: 01626
835285. Open all year, most
days. Free.
**Yelverton Paperweight
Centre**
4 Buckland Terrace, Leg O'
Mutton, Yelverton. Tel: 01822
854250. Open Apr–Oct & Dec,
daily except 25 Dec; weekends
other months.

**SPECIAL INTEREST FOR
CHILDREN**

The following places may be of
interest to visitors with children.
Unless otherwise stated, there
will be an admission charge.
**Buckfast Butterflies and
Dartmoor Otter Sanctuary**
Buckfastleigh. Tel: 01364
642916. Open Mar–Oct, daily.
National Marine Aquarium
The Barbican, Plymouth. Tel:
01752 220084. Open all year,
daily, except 25 Dec.
Pennywell
Buckfastleigh. Tel: 01364
642023. Open all year, daily.
Plymouth Dome
The Hoe, Plymouth. Tel: 01752
603300/600608. Open early Apr
to mid-Oct.
**Teign Valley Glass and
House of Marbles**
The Old Pottery, Pottery Road,
Bovey Tracey. Tel: 01626
8353258. Open all year, most
days. Free.

Shopping

Ashburton
Antiques

Okehampton
Pannier Market, Sat.
Plymouth
The Barbican, crafts, antiques
and galleries.
Tavistock
Pannier Market, Tue–Sat.
Victorian Fair and Aladdin's Cave
first and last Sat in the month.
Tel: 01822 611003.
Crafts 2nd & 3rd Sats in month.

LOCAL SPECIALITIES

Clotted Cream
Available everywhere. Many
shops will dispatch cream by
post.
Crafts
Devon Guild of Craftsmen,
Riverside Mill, Bovey Tracey.
Tel: 01626 832223.
Roundhouse Craft Centre,
Buckland in the Moor,
Ashburton. Tel: 01364 653234.
Glass
Teign Valley Glass and House of
Marbles, The Old Pottery,
Pottery Road, Bovey Tracey.
Shop with samples and seconds.
Tel: 01626 835285.
West Country Cheeses
Shop in the Pannier Market,
Market Road, Tavistock.
Tel: 01822 615035.

The Performing Arts

Barbican Theatre
Castle Street, Plymouth.
Tel: 01752 267131.
Plymouth Arts Centre
38 Looe Street, Plymouth.
Tel: 01752 206114.
Plymouth Pavilions
Millbay Road, Plymouth.
Tel: 01752 229922.
**Theatre Royal/Drum
Theatre**
Royal Parade, Plymouth.
Tel: 01752 668282/267222.

**Sports, Activities
and the Outdoors**

ANGLING
Fly
Drakelands, Hemerdon, nr
Plymouth.
Tel: 01752 344691.
Milemead Fisheries, Mill Hill,
Tavistock.
Tel: 01822 610888.

Roadford Lake, Lewdown, Okehampton.
Tel: 01837 871565.
Tavistock Trout Farm and Fishery, Mount Tavy, Parkwood Road, Tavistock.
Tel: 01822 615441.
Coarse
Kennick, Tottiford and Trenchford Reservoirs, Bovey Tracey. Tel: 01837 871565.

BOAT TRIPS
Plymouth
Trips from Phoenix Wharf and Mayflower Steps, Barbican to view The Hoe, Drake's Island, The Breakwater, the Dockyards and RN ships, also to Calstock, Morwellham, Weir Head, River Yealm and Looe when tide permits.

BUS TOURS
Plymouth Citybus runs Guide Friday open top bus tours from Easter to October, providing guided tours of the city.
Tel: 01752 222221.

COUNTRY PARKS, FORESTS AND NATURE RESERVES
Abbeyford Woods.
Tel: 01392 832262.
Bellever, High Dartmoor.
Tel: 01392 832262.
Cann, north of Plympton.
Tel: 01392 832262.
Chudleigh Knighton Heath, nr Bovey Tracey
Tel: 01392 79244.
Dart Valley Reserve, Widecombe.
Tel: 01392 79244
Denham, off the A386 Plymouth to Tavistock road.
Tel: 01392 832262.
Dunsford Woods Reserve.
Tel: 01392 79244
Fernworthy, High Dartmoor.
Tel: 01392 832262.
Lydford, between Okehampton and Tavistock.
Tel: 01409 221692.
River Dart Country Park.
Tel: 01364 652511.
Yarner Wood, near Bovey Tracey.
Tel: 01626 832330.

CYCLING
Information on cycle routes is available from local Tourist Information Centres; also visit www.devon.gov.uk/tourism/ncn
Dedicated BikeBuses no longer operate, but it is hoped that buses on the route between Plymouth and Barnstaple via Yelverton, Tavistock, Okehampton, Hatherleigh, Torrington and Bideford, will be adapted to carry up to four cycles. For further information contact DevonBus Line Tel: 01392 382800.

CYCLE HIRE
Ashburton
Devon Pedallers, Mountain Bike Centre Ltd, A38 Business Park.
Tel: 01364 654080.
Plymouth
Plymouth Cycle Hire. Tel: 01752 258944.
Tavistock
Tavistock Cycles and Hire Centres, Paddons Row, Brook Street.
Tel: 01822 617630.
Yelverton
Burrator Bicycles, Peek Hill Farm, Dousland, Yelverton. Tel: 01822 854808.

GOLF COURSES
Moretonhampstead
Manor House Hotel and Golf Club. Tel: 01647 440961. Book in advance.
Okehampton
Okehampton Golf Club, off Tors Road. Tel: 01837 52113.
Tavistock
Hurdwick Golf Club, Tavistock Hamlets. Tel 01822 612746.
Tavistock Golf Club, Down Road. Tel: 01822 612344.
Yelverton
Yelverton Golf Club, Golf Links Road. Tel: 01822 852824.

HORSE-RIDING
Okehampton
Lydford House Riding Stables, Lydford House Hotel.
Tel: 01822 820321.
Wembury
Wembury Riding School, Church Wood Estate.
Tel: 01752 862676.
Widecombe in the Moor
Shilstone Rocks Riding & Trekking Centre.
Tel: 01364 621281.

SAILING
Plymouth
Plymouth Sailing School, Queen Anne's Battery Marina, Coxside.
Tel: 01752 671142.

SKIING
Plymouth
Plymouth Ski Centre. The complex has 3 slopes and a toboggan run. Tel: 01752 600220.

WATERSPORTS
Roadford Lake, Okehampton.
Tel: 01409 211507.

Annual Events and Customs

Buckfastleigh
River Dart Sponsored Struggle Raft Race, from Buckfastleigh to Totnes, October.
Okehampton
Okehampton and District Carnival, mid-October.
Plymouth
Double-handed Transatlantic Race, Plymouth, early June.
Plymouth Navy Days, biennial event (alternates with Portsmouth). August Bank Holiday weekend.
Tavistock
Carnival, early July.
Goosey Fair, mid-October.
Dickensian Evening mid-December.
Widecombe in the Moor
Widecombe Fair 2nd Tuesday mid-September.

The checklists give details of just some of the facilities within the area covered by this guide. Further information can be obtained from Tourist Information Centres.

The English Riviera and The South Hams

In 1983 the resorts of Brixham, Torquay and Paignton, a long-established seaside playground, were re-launched as The English Riviera, an exotic, yet still very English alternative to going abroad. Torquay comes closest to achieving the sophisticated image; Paignton is more kiss-me-quick than 'je ne sais quoi', while Brixham remains an unspoilt fishing port. The South Hams is very different world – an agricultural  region studded with small villages. The countryside is particularly beautiful, especially along the River Dart and around the Kingsbridge estuary. In Totnes and Dartmouth it has two of England's most charming small towns.

BERRY POMEROY CASTLE Map ref SX8261

Berry Pomeroy is one of Devon's best-known castles, famous for its romantic ruined ivy-dripping appearance and for its many ghosts. Certainly many of the Pomeroys, who settled here after the Norman Conquest, met violent deaths and so too did the builder of much of the present castle, Edward Seymour, who was executed in 1552 shortly after he had acquired Berry Pomeroy. His designs were never completed, the castle was partially destroyed in a fire and by the mid-18th century it was deserted. English Heritage are now the custodians.

It's an unusual design, being a mansion within a castle. Inside the gatehouse and massive curtain wall are the ruins of a great Tudor house, with a hall nearly 50 feet (15m) long. The earliest parts of the castle go back to the 14th century and a 15th-century fresco painting also remains from the Pomeroy period. The other delight of visiting Berry Pomeroy is its superb site, high on a wooded hillside overlooking a glorious deep valley and stream.

Among the ghosts who are reputed to inhabit the ruins of Berry Pomeroy Castle are a daughter of the castle and her secret paramour, who also happened to be an enemy of her family. They were discovered in each other's arms one night by her brother, who killed them both, so that they are now destined to remain just out of reach of true happiness for eternity.

CLOTTED CREAM

One of the most popular West Country experiences is to partake of a clotted cream tea, and invitations to do so are found at regular intervals along most streets and country lanes. The delicious main ingredient, the clotted cream, is produced from milk with the highest cream content. It is left to stand in a pan for between 12 and 24 hours, then gently heated (never boiled) until a solid ring of clotted cream has formed around the edge. The pan is then left covered in a cool place for another 24 hours before the cream is skimmed from the top with a slotted spoon. Real Devon cream teas substitute Devonshire Splits, a kind of sweet bread roll, for the usual scones.

HISTORIC LANDINGS

The historical link between Brixham and Drake's famous 16th-century flagship is rather tenuous, though he did put in here in 1588 with his captured galleon, *Capitana*, from the Spanish Armada. A century later, William of Orange, soon to be William III, also came ashore here in order to claim the throne from James II. A statue on the front marks the landing.

A full-size model of Drake's ship, the **Golden Hind***, in which he sailed around the world, is a crowd-pleaser in Brixham's busy harbour*

BRIXHAM Map ref SX9255

Brixham is the least commercialised part of Torbay, with a pretty harbour surrounded by some fine old buildings and a handful of colour-washed cottages. Here the fish-and-chip shops, cheap eating houses and other typical seaside outlets seem, at least, to have made an effort to blend in with their old surroundings.

This is very much a seafaring community, as evidenced by the replica of the *Golden Hind* in the harbour (open to the public) and the Aquarium and Trawling Exhibition on the dockside. By 1851 Brixham had one of the largest fisheries in all England, the trawler was virtually invented here, but steam-powered boats heralded the decline of the fleet, which by 1945 was almost non-existent. Fishing continues today but only on a small scale. The Brixham Museum on New Road traces the ebb and flow of the town's maritime fortunes over nine centuries of seafaring; you can get right up to date by visiting the working marina next to the harbour.

There are some fine beaches near by – St Mary's Bay is large and sandy but the rest are small, shingle or pebble shores and are relatively peaceful and undeveloped. Just to the east of town lies Berry Head Country Park, a splendid nature reserve, ideal for walking and for enjoying the views from the headland. The remains of a huge Napoleonic fort can also be visited here.

While the Burgh Island Hotel is linked with the jet-set, a humbler trade may be found at the venerable Pilchard Inn

BURGH ISLAND   Map ref SX6544

Burgh Island is one of the curiosities of Devon – a tiny rock covering just 28 acres – and from the headland at Bigbury-on-Sea you can see all its points of interest. The largest structure, the rather unprepossessing box-shaped building is, surprisingly, a luxury hotel. Just to the right is the much humbler, but atmospheric abode of the Pilchard Inn. Until the mid-19th century Burgh Island was a prosperous pilchard-fishing community and the 14th-century inn was a fisherman's cottage. High above it is the Huer's Hut. A lookout was stationed here and when the great shoals of pilchards were spotted he would raise a hue and cry – hence the name.

Burgh Island is in fact only an island at high tide. At other times you can walk or drive – 'England 282 metres' says the sign! The most novel way to arrive however is at high tide, aboard the extraordinary Burgh Island sea tractor, which, with its passenger compartment raised high above the waves, can safely cross in up to 7 feet (2m) of water.

DARTINGTON   Map ref SX7862

The Dartington Estate was founded in 1925 when Leonard and Dorothy Elmhirst bought 14th-century Dartington Hall and gardens (the largest medieval house in the west of England) as part of a project of regenerating rural life in this part of Devon. The house, now brilliantly renovated, is part of a conference and arts centre which promotes one of the best programmes of music, theatre, films and arts courses in the southwest of England. When not in use the spectacular Great Hall is open to the public and its beautiful 25-acre gardens are open daily.

The Dartington name has been made world-famous by the project's most glittering success, its Dartington Crystal glass factory located at Great Torrington (see page 40). Another high profile project is the restoration of Morwellham Quay (see page 64).

The neighbouring Dartington Cider Press Centre is the

CELEBRITY VISITORS

The Burgh Island Hotel was built in 1929 by the eccentric millionaire Archibald Nettlefold, who owned the island and used the hotel as a guest house for his friends and associates. These included the Duke of Windsor and Mrs Simpson, Noel Coward and Agatha Christie, who wrote here prolifically (*Evil Under the Sun* is set on the island). In more recent times Kirk Douglas and The Beatles have also secreted themselves here. If you want to admire the splendid art deco interior of the hotel today you'll have to book a meal or cream tea.

MARITIME TRADITIONS
Dartmouth has been an important port since early medieval times when the Normans started trading with their homeland. Richard the Lionheart and the Crusaders departed from here and in the Middle Ages Dartmouth enjoyed considerable trade with Europe. By the 17th century, however, Bristol and London had become the major trade centres and Dartmouth retained only its naval duties. The famous Royal Britannia Naval College, high above the river, has trained the seafaring elite since 1905, including members of the present royal family. There are guided tours of the college during the summer.

DARTMOUTH BY SAIL OR STEAM
The best way of exploring the Dart (and of getting a sailor's-eye view of Dartmouth) is to take a boat trip. As you sail upstream you will pass the charming village of Dittisham and Greenway House, in which Agatha Christie lived and wrote many of her novels. Another way of seeing this beautiful valley is to take the passenger ferry to Kingswear and board the Paignton & Dartmouth Steam Railway. This runs for 7 miles (11.2km) stopping at Churston, Goodrington and Paignton (see page 88). There are also tickets available which combine train and boat.

Regular small ferries ply the short distance between Dartmouth, with its wide promenade, and steeply-set Kingswear, opposite

finest small-scale shopping centre and exhibition showcase in the whole region, with very high quality contemporary crafts, farm foods, plants, books, kitchenware, Dartington Glass and much more, drawing from both within and beyond the Estate. The centre enjoys a bucolic setting around an old cider press, with craft demonstrations and street entertainment.

DARTMOUTH Map ref SX8751

The ancient town and deepwater port of Dartmouth enjoys an unrivalled setting at the mouth of the picturesque River Dart, with steep green hills to either side and a busy, colourful estuary. The Embankment is a lovely uncluttered promenade, free of tourist trappings, and the colourful houses of Kingswear, many built for Dartmouth's wealthy merchants and sea captains, dot the far bank. Neither major road nor railway link has ever reached Dartmouth and this has undoubtedly helped the centre of town – a tiny web of criss-crossing cobbled streets and narrow alleyways – to retain its ancient atmosphere.

In the very centre is the Boatfloat, a charming inner harbour only accessible to small craft. Near the Boatfloat is Thomas Newcomen's Atmospheric Steam Engine, a 'nodding donkey' type engine, invented in 1712, which is claimed to be the first ever successful steam engine. Also just off the Boatfloat, on Duke Street, is the 17th-century Butterwalk, a four-storey arcaded house encrusted with wood carvings, its three upper floors supported by eleven granite pillars. It now houses shops and the delightful small Dartmouth Museum, with a whole flotilla of model ships and some original 17th-century plaster and panelling. Further along Duke Street is the old cobbled market square and building, erected in 1829, now home to various permanent shops but still the site of the weekly markets.

Two buildings which have survived from the 14th century are The Cherub pub, Dartmouth's oldest building (c1380) and Agincourt House, now home to a coffee shop. The most famous part of town, however, is the charming cobbled quayside of Bayard's Cove, which featured regularly in the famous television series, *The Onedin Line*. The Pilgrim Fathers put into Bayard's Cove in 1620 en route to the New World and some five centuries earlier the Crusaders departed from here. You can explore the shell of a small fortress, built in 1510 to protect the harbour entrance.

Near the mouth of the river is Dartmouth Castle, a small fortification built in 1481 to stop sea raids on Dartmouth. It was added to in the 16th and 18th centuries and was the first to be designed specifically with gunports in mind, thus giving its cannons maximum angle of fire. The views from here are superb and as the castle was never harmed, it still retains its ancient atmosphere.

Dawlish developed as a genteel resort from the early 19th century, and received a boost with the arrival of the railway in 1848

DAWLISH WARREN NATURE RESERVE
Over 450 plant species are protected at this 500-acre nature reserve including a number of orchids and the famous Warren crocus, only found here. A large hide looks out over the estuary, where oystercatchers, terns and sanderling can be seen. In mid-winter the estuary is host to Brent geese and a flock of wintering avocets. There is a visitor centre from where guided walks are conducted.

DAWLISH   Map ref SX9576

This pleasantly old-fashioned seaside resort, once the haunt of Charles Dickens and Jane Austen, is famous for its landscaped gardens, known as The Lawn. These stretch back from the front, flanked by two peaceful streams which are home to black swans. Around here are some fine Regency, Georgian and Victorian buildings, and there is a small local museum on Barton Terrace. One curious feature is the way that the mainline train runs right alongside the beach. As many old local pictures confirm, this was a stirring sight in the days of steam and for most people it was the only way to get to the seaside. Today's thunderous locomotives, however, are likely to shake your sandcastles to their foundations!

To the north is Dawlish Warren and a 1½-mile (2.4-km) long dune system which incorporates a large nature reserve. There is a pleasant coastal walk to the Warren from the centre of Dawlish.

KINGSBRIDGE   Map ref SX7344

Despite its modest size Kingsbridge has been known as 'the capital of the South Hams' since the 13th century, when it was first granted its market charter, and ever since then has been the regional market centre. Steep Fore Street, lined with speciality shops, rises up from the Quay where there is a splendid leisure centre. This is the highest point of the picturesque Kingsbridge Estuary, the flooded river valley on which Salcombe also lies, and an enjoyable boat trip links the two towns in summer.

For many visitors the highlight of Kingsbridge is the excellent Cookworthy Museum of Rural Life in South

Devon, in Fore Street. This is dedicated to William Cookworthy, a Quaker, born in Kingsbridge in 1705 and a pioneer in the English porcelain industry. The collection, set in a 17th-century schoolhouse, is one of the best of its kind in the region. It reflects many aspects of Devon life throughout the centuries and includes examples of a Victorian kitchen and an Edwardian pharmacy, plus a large farm gallery in a walled garden.

Towards the top of Fore Street is a colonnaded 16th-century shambles of shops, a fine 15th-century church and the Town Hall, with its peculiarly shaped 19th-century clock tower. Explore, too, the picturesque narrow back streets and passages.

NEWTON ABBOT   Map ref SX8571

Newton Abbot has been a market and crossroads town for centuries; first in medieval times on the main road between the major ports of Dartmouth and Exeter; later when granite from Haytor was shipped to London, then most importantly in 1846 when the railway arrived. The town became the centre of the Great Western Railway locomotive works, employing over 600 people, and many of the neat terraces built to accommodate the workforce remain today. Newton Abbot's other claim to fame is its National Hunt horse-racing course and this, along with much other local history, is covered in the Newton Abbot Museum on St Paul's Road.

The most fascinating attraction in town is Tucker's Maltings. This is Britain's only working malthouse open to the public (it produces enough malt to make 15 million pints of beer a year) and a lively guided tour covers the process of malting. You'll remember the evocative smells for a long time and adults can sample the beer of the brewery that shares the premises.

Southwest of the town, off the A381 Totnes road, is Bradley Manor (National Trust), a small 11th-century manor house set in woodlands and meadows.

A ROYAL DECLARATION
At the centre of Newton Abbot is the ancient tower of St Leonard's, all that remains of the medieval church. Beside here a plaque marks the spot where the first declaration of William III, Prince of Orange, was read as he made his way from Brixham to London to assume the English throne. He stayed overnight in Forde House, an early 17th-century house to the southeast of town.

The tower of St Leonard's is all that remains of a medieval church in the main street of Newton Abbot

A steam train vies for visitors' attention with the excitements of the water park and the delights of the sheltered beach at Paignton

ST JOHN'S CHURCH
Paignton's St John's Church, which dates from the 15th century, is an unusual blend of red sandstone and white Beer stone. The headless angels inside were damaged by the Puritans in the 17th century and there is also a grisly skeleton.

PAIGNTON   Map ref SX8860

Around a century ago Paignton was described as 'a neat and improving village and bathing place'. It remains a popular bathing place but is no longer a village, and, because of its garish amusement arcades, cheap eating houses and discount stores, is often regarded as a poor relation to neighbouring Torquay. Paignton, however, is unabashed, and performs its role of cheap holiday provider very effectively. The beaches, some of the best in the south-west, are the main draw, particularly Goodrington Sands which features the region's largest water park. In high summer it can be unbearably crowded, but there are many more beaches of varying character in the vicinity.

Although the town may appear devoid of high culture, there are historic houses to visit. Oldway Mansion, built by Isaac Singer (founder of the sewing-machine empire) in 1874, is now used as council offices, but the best rooms are open to the public. Just outside town, near Marldon, is Compton Castle (National Trust), a fortified manor house built between 1340 and 1520 and home to the descendants of Sir Humphrey Gilbert, who colonised Newfoundland. Paignton Zoo, in 75 verdant acres one mile (1.6km) from the town, is one of the largest zoos in the country, with all the usual favourites – lions, tigers, elephants, rhinos, monkeys and giraffes. For many visitors, however, the finest thing to come out of Paignton is the Paignton and Dartmouth Steam Railway which steams along a delightful scenic line to Kingswear along the Dart Estuary (see Dartmouth page 84).

SALCOMBE Map ref SX7439

The great blue saucer of Salcombe Bay, aflutter with white triangular sails, surrounded by the green hills of the South Hams and fringed by golden pocket handkerchief beaches, is one of South Devon's finest sights. Salcombe is one of the largest yachting centres in England and several old wharf houses are workshops for boat makers and marine engineers.

The tiny golden beach of North Sands is adjacent to the picturesque ruin of Salcombe Castle/Fort Charles, which was built in 1544 to protect against French and Spanish raiders but destroyed during the Civil War. Continue on to South Sands and Splat Cove or alternatively catch a ferry to one of the beaches on the other side of the bay.

One and a half miles (2.4km) southwest of Salcombe, at Sharpitor, is Overbecks Museum and Garden (National Trust), a charming Edwardian house largely dedicated to local maritime affairs. Overbecks' beautiful 6-acre garden, set high above the estuary, is full of rare and exotic specimens which revel in the area's mild micro-climate and is worth a visit for its views alone.

SLAPTON Map ref SX8245

Slapton Sands is an uncommercialised 2-mile (3.2-km) long windswept shingle ridge, a favourite spot for walking. Slapton Ley, divided from the beach by the road, is a freshwater lake, famous for its wildfowl (see Walk on page 90). This is a National Nature Reserve and a public hide, for birdwatching, is situated in the Torcross car park.

The village of Slapton (½ mile/0.8km) inland and not to be confused with Torcross at the southernmost part of Slapton Sands) features a fine medieval church. The impressive tower to the north of the church is the remains of a College of Chantry Priests, founded in 1373. Just north of Slapton Sands is the unspoiled sandy cove of Blackpool Sands, rated by many as the best beach in the South Hams.

D-DAY TRAINING

As part of the preparations for the D-Day landings in 1944, American troops used Slapton Sands for manoeuvres on account of their similarity to the Normandy beaches. Tragically, while training, a convoy was attacked by German torpedo boats with the loss of 749 lives. An American Sherman tank in the car park at Torcross is a memorial to this event. The tank was lost from a landing craft during the attack but was remarkably salvaged from 65 feet (20m) of water in 1984.

A memorial at Slapton Ley commemorates US servicemen who lost their lives near by while preparing for the D-Day landings in France

Around Slapton Ley

A varied and interesting walk incorporating undulating coast and field paths, peaceful narrow lanes, a nature trail and a level path overlooking Slapton Ley, Devon's largest natural freshwater lake. It is well worth taking a pair of binoculars to view the abundant birdlife.

Time: Allow 4 hours. Distance: 6½ miles (10.5km).
Location: 7 miles (11.3km) south of Dartmouth.
Start: Slapton Sands car park beside the A379.
(OS grid ref: SX829442.)
OS Map: Outdoor Leisure 20 (South Devon)
1:25,000.
See Key to Walks on page 121.

ROUTE DIRECTIONS

From the car park either follow the shingle path above the beach, or cross the road to the path beside **Slapton Ley** and head south in the direction of Torcross. At the **Sherman Tank (memorial)**, join the old road beside the sea wall in

A Sherman tank completes the memorial at Slapton Ley

Torcross, and continue to the end at Torcross Apartment Hotel. Climb the steps to the left, signed 'Coastal Path', pausing at the top to take in the magnificent view towards the Dart estuary. Follow the yellow arrowed (circular walk) zigzag path uphill, eventually passing though a gate into a field. Proceed up a defined path to a further gate then descend on a narrow stony path skirting an old slate quarry. On nearing the bottom near **Beesands**, turn right, following the sign for 'Widewell'.

Shortly, climb a waymarked stile, keep left-handed through pasture and soon join a track along the field edge. Do not go through the gate ahead, instead cross the two stiles on the right and enter woodland. Keep to the main path as it bears right with woodland fringe around **Widdicombe Estate** and pass a pair of cottages.

Turn right along the metalled driveway, then soon take the arrowed path right,

signposted 'Widewell', and pass through a kissing gate into a field. Head downhill to another kissing gate and continue ahead down a little-used, grass-centred lane for about half a mile (0.8km) to Stokenham and the A379.

Cross over, pass between the pub and church, and at the junction just before the Tradesman's Arms, turn right. Go uphill to Kiln Lane. Turn right, then immediately left by Kiln Lodge and follow the high-banked lane to the farm buildings at Frittiscombe. Where the road bears left, turn right in front of a high wall, signed 'Scrubs Lane to Deer Bridge' and soon ascend the track to the road. Turn right downhill for about three quarters of a mile (1.2km), enjoying cameo views to the Ley. Cross Deer Bridge, then in 50 yards (46m) turn right on a path, signed 'Marsh Lane'. Follow this track beside reed beds (can be wet and muddy) and in half a mile (0.8km) reach a fingerpost and junction of paths.

Join the permissive route through the Nature Reserve and follow the boardwalk through the reedbeds to a T-junction of paths. Turn right, signed 'Slapton Sands via Nature Trail' and keep to the defined path along the edge of the Ley, passing the warden's hut, to a gate and lane. Turn right across Slapton Bridge back to the car park.

POINTS OF INTEREST

Slapton Ley and Nature Reserve
Separated from the sea by a narrow shingle bar, this area of freshwater, marsh and reedbeds provides excellent feeding and breeding grounds for a rich and varied wildlife. It is an important resting place for migratory birds in spring

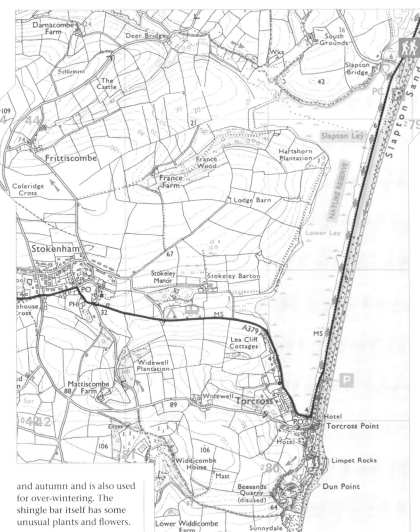

and autumn and is also used for over-wintering. The shingle bar itself has some unusual plants and flowers.

Sherman Tank Memorial

Salvaged from the sea in 1984, the tank stands as a memorial to the American troops killed off Slapton Sands during 'Exercise Tiger', the preparation for the D-Day landings in 1944.

Torcross

This exposed little village is built partly on the shingle bar and is periodically battered by gales. Until the pilchard shoals disappeared from the southwest coast, Torcross was the most easterly village to engage in this trade.

Beesands

During the 18th and 19th centuries, soft blue slate was extracted from the quarry in this tiny fishing village and carried away by sea.

Widdicombe

The 400-acre Widdicombe Estate dates back to the days of its Saxon settlement. Captain Cook is believed to have stayed here on his return from Tahiti, and during World War II Widdicombe was commandeered by General Eisenhower for use as the Combined Services Headquarters.

DISAPPEARING HALLSANDS
The village of Hallsands, northwest of Start Point, now just a hotel and a couple of cottages, was once a prosperous fishing community of 37 houses. In the early years of this century its protective offshore shingle bank was dredged to provide materials for building dockyards in Plymouth. As a result of this the beach level dropped and in 1917 storms destroyed all but one of the houses. Today Hallsands is a popular and picturesque shingle sunbathing beach (swimming can be dangerous) and traces of the lost village can be seen a couple of minutes' walk behind the present hotel.

START POINT Map ref SX8337

Start Point is the dramatic southwesterly tip of the South Hams with cliffs rising over 100 feet (30.5m) high. On the south side they are almost sheer and streaked by quartz veins which run through the dark rock. A lighthouse (tours available) warns shipping off the dangerous bank known as the Skerries. In Elizabethan times pirates were hung in chains here as a warning to other lawless seafarers.

From Start Point the coast path heads west to Prawle Point, the southernmost extremity of Devon. The latter, lashed by the full fury of the waves in stormy weather, has been chiselled and chipped into an almost vertical drop beneath the coastguard look-out station.

TEIGNMOUTH Map ref SX9473

The bright red cliffs with a verdant fringe and the red sand beaches of Teignmouth (pronounced Tin-muth) make this a distinctive seafront, complete with an old-fashioned pier. The town became a fashionable resort in the late 18th and early 19th centuries and if you look along Powderham Terrace or The Den, or just up above the fronts of the many cafés and tourist shops, you will see that it retains a good deal of its Georgian and early Victorian architecture. The Quays are full of character; this is the old harbour area which has for centuries shipped huge quantities of Bovey ball clay and Dartmoor granite. A small fishing fleet also operates from here. You can learn more about the town's local and maritime history in the museum in French Street.

A narrow bridge connects Teignmouth to the pretty village of Shaldon, where the houses, many of which are Georgian, are packed so closely together that the only sensible way of visiting is by ferry from Teignmouth, a service that dates back to Elizabethan times. There's a fine church to see but the favourite attraction is the charming Shaldon Wildlife Trust. It is a breeding centre

The view along the sea-front to the tall tower of St James's Church, Teignmouth

for rare and endangered species of small mammals, exotic birds and reptiles and because of its tiny size many of its inmates are very tame. Close by, the erroneously named 'Smuggler's tunnel' leads to Shaldon's own beach, the Ness, backed by a bold red cliff. From the top of here there are marvellous views of Teignmouth and the Teign estuary.

TORQUAY   Map ref SX9164

Torquay is South Devon at its most continental – a balmy climate, palm trees bathed in coloured lights and millionaires' yachts basking in the marina. There's even a large number of foreign visitors to add an exotic chatter to the town. Yet this is also the capital of the 'English Riviera' – the birthplace of Agatha Christie; more recently the fictional setting of the BBC television series *Fawlty Towers* (don't expect to find the actual location here; the series was filmed elsewhere).

From humble beginnings as a fishing village the town's resort career began during Napoleonic times, and by the Victorian era its mild winters were attracting consumptives and fashionable visitors on doctors' orders. By 1850 it was proclaiming itself 'Queen of the Watering Holes' and today it is the country's second most popular seaside resort after Blackpool.

The centre of town is the lively marina and harbour, including the listed copper-domed Edwardian Pavilion which now houses an excellent shopping centre.

With houses opening straight on to the beach, The Quay reveals a practical side to Teignmouth's past

A FLAVOUR OF HISTORIC SHALDON
Every Wednesday in summer Shaldon turns the clock back to 1785 (denoting the approximate age of many of its houses) with traders dressed in period costume, special craft stalls and evening entertainment.

Torquay's palm trees and elegant Pavilion confirm that Riviera touch in this fashionable south coast resort

PREHISTORIC RESIDENTS

As far as we know, the earliest human occupation of these islands was around 400,000 years ago and Kent's Cavern is one of only two sites in the whole country that provide evidence to this effect (the other is a modern quarry in Somerset). Here at Torquay a layer of conglomerate limestone revealed simple tools and evidence of stone working from that date, as well as the even earlier remains of animals such as sabre-toothed tigers, mammoths and bears.

Eastwards the cliffs rise up to Daddy Hole Plain, a great chasm in the cliff where the plain meets the sea, and the views from here are superb. Continue east to the point at Hope's Nose for more sea panoramas.

The beaches, though not as broad and sandy as those at neighbouring Paignton, are numerous and well spread apart, which helps to dissipate the crowds. The most attractive of the major beaches is Oddicombe, with its picturesque backdrop of steep sandstone cliffs topped by lush woodland. The descent is steep and a cliff railway runs down 720 feet (220m) to the shingle below.

The Oddicombe/Babbacombe area is also home to Torquay's best tourist attractions. Kents Caverns form one of the most important prehistoric sites in Europe, where a fascinating and atmospheric half a mile (0.8km) guided tour takes you back through two million years of history, with many natural spectacular rock formations. More cave finds can be seen at the Torquay Museum on Babbacombe Road.

Another excellent wet-weather option, in the charming St Marychurch parish, is Bygones, a life-size re-creation of a Victorian street, illustrating shops and dwellings, including an ironmongers, grocers, sweet shop and apothecary, with minute nostalgic details right down to authentic smells. Visit the giant model railway and the walk through Trench Experience with the sights, sounds and smells of World War I.

Torquay's favourite attraction, also in St Marychurch,

is its Model Village, an outstanding piece of design, full of interest for everyone, and regarded as a masterpiece of miniature landscape gardening. A nice sense of typically English humour pervades the village, with the minuscule Lord Elpusall waiting to show you his one-twelfth size stately home. Visit again by night (summer only), to see the miniature illuminations which also feature a spectacular Close Encounters-style spacecraft.

Next to the harbour is Torre Abbey, from where the town derives its name. Originally constructed in the 12th century, the abbey was dissolved and subsumed into a 16th-century mansion, itself remodelled in the Georgian period. It now holds the municipal art gallery, featuring 19th-century artists and a local history collection. In the grounds are monastic ruins, the well-preserved abbey gatehouse, exotic gardens and a splendid 12th-century tithe barn, known as the Spanish Barn, since it was used in 1588 to hold some 400 Armada prisoners captured by Sir Francis Drake.

Just one mile (1.6km) west from the centre of town is the picture-postcard village of Cockington, a crossroads gathering of thatched cottages with an old smithy, the village stocks, a mill pond and working waterwheel. Despite the number of summer visitors and the inevitable tea shops that have sprung up, this is still a beautiful and largely unspoiled place. The grounds and gardens of 19th-century Cockington Court are open to the public and include a craft centre and gallery.

THE MYSTERIOUS CASE OF THE TORQUAY WRITER
One of Britain's best-loved and most successful authors, Agatha Christie, was born at Barton in Torquay and frequently returned to the county of her birth. Her books have been translated into more than a hundred languages and there have been countless film and TV adaptations, but she maintained her own air of mystery and little is known about her private life. The brochure, *Agatha Christie's Riviera*, highlights 26 locations associated with the author, including the museum and Torre Abbey. It is available from the tourist information office.

The town has justly kept its place at the top of the league of Britain's seaside resorts

Fore Street, Totnes's main shopping thoroughfare, is distinguished by its fine East Gate Arch

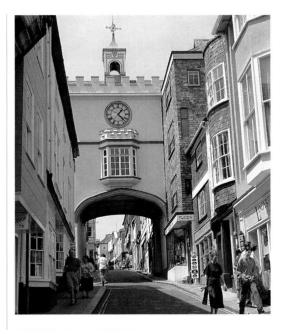

TWO ANCIENT WATERING HOLES

At the top of Fore Street, in Totnes, continue up into the Narrows – the reason for its name is obvious – then turn left into Leechwell Street and you will come to the town's oldest pub, the picturesque 17th-century Kingsbridge Inn. To the left a narrow passage, Leechwell Lane, runs down to an ancient well with three granite troughs. This was once thought to have had medicinal properties and was specially administered by town wardens.

TOTNES Map ref SX8060

This ancient picturesque town set high on a hill above the River Dart is one of South Devon's gems. At the bottom of the town the old Steamer Quay, once a thriving river port, is still home to many working boats, while pleasure trips also run from here to Dartmouth. (Another excellent way of arriving is via the South Devon Railway steam train from Buckfastleigh along the beautiful Dart valley, see page 54.)

From the Quay steep, claustrophobic Fore Street climbs into the centre of Totnes passing several fine 16th- and 17th-century merchants' houses. Their wealth was established in medieval and Tudor times when the export of wool and tin from Dartmoor made Totnes one of England's richest towns. One of the finest buildings is the Elizabethan House, beautifully restored to house the lively local museum. Partly timbered and dating from 1575, it features furniture, domestic objects, toys, dolls, railway paraphernalia and a Victorian grocer's shop. One room is dedicated to Charles Babbage who is regarded as a pioneer of modern computers. Continue up the hill and it becomes apparent why Totnes has declared itself to be the 'health-food capital of the West Country', with a plethora of wholefood shops and eating places. But if you turn right just past the handsome Tudor East Gate Arch, into the charming Ramparts Walk, you will come to the Guildhall, a preserved 16th-century building where you can see the old jail and a table where Oliver Cromwell sat in 1646. Perhaps most remarkable of all is the fact that the present town council still meets here.

Back on Fore Street seek out the pillared shop arcades, or shambles, of the Butterwalk and Poultry Walk which once sheltered the markets which were held here. A lively local market is held opposite the Butterwalk every Friday and Saturday, while on Tuesdays in summer it plays host to a costumed Elizabethan charity market. There are more costumes to be seen inside the Butterwalk at the Devonshire Collection of Period Costume, housed in the superbly renovated Bogan House of *c*1500. At the top of the hill is Totnes Castle (English Heritage), a perfect example of a small Norman motte and bailey fortress, with wonderful views over the town and the Dart. On Coronation Road you will find Totnes Town Mill which houses the Tourist Information Centre, a restored Victorian waterwheel and mill machinery, and an excellent interpretative exhibition showing the development of Totnes.

Bowden House, one mile (1.6km) west, was built in 1510, but much altered in 1704 and has some fine Queen Anne detail. It's an entertaining place with costumed guides and an interesting photographic museum, but trades rather heavily on its 'haunted house' theme in the pursuit of the coach party trade.

YEALMPTON Map ref SX5851

Yealmpton is a small village on the edge of the South Hams between Modbury and Plymouth. The parish church of St Bartholomew is well worth exploring for a number of reasons. In the churchyard is a Roman pillar, the font is Saxon and highly polished marble from Kitley Quarries (part of the Kitley House estate) features in the walls, chancel screen and altar table. St Bartholomew's was rebuilt in 1850 and Sir John Betjeman called it the 'most amazing' Victorian church in the county.

Kitley House is not open to the public but its quarries and part of its estate have become Kitley Caves and Country Park featuring illuminated caves and a museum.

OLD MOTHER HUBBARD
Yealmpton, or 'Yampton' as it is pronounced, is the home of Old Mother Hubbard, so to speak. The famous rhyme was written locally in 1805 and the lady in question is thought to have been a housekeeper at the local manor, Kitley House. Old Mother Hubbard's Cottage, to which she retired in the late 1700s, is a perfect 16th-century Devon cob and thatch building at the east end of the village. Rather ironically it is now a restaurant.

You're unlikely to find a bare cupboard at Mother Hubbard's little white cottage today

Cornworthy and Tranquil Bow Creek

A beautiful rural walk that explores tranquil wooded creeks and sleepy villages in an unspoilt part of the rolling South Hams countryside. Good, well-waymarked paths and green lanes.

Time: Approx. 2½ hours. Distance: 4 miles (6.4km).
Location: 3 miles (4.8km) south of Totnes.
Start: Roadside parking near Cornworthy village hall or in Hunters Lodge Inn car park (with permission).
(OS grid ref: SX829555.)
OS Map: Outdoor Leisure 20 (South Devon)
1:25,000.
See Key to Walks on page 121.

ROUTE DIRECTIONS

Facing the parish hall and the church, follow the footpath marker left through a farmyard, soon to turn right past Cornworthy Court and go through gates on to a track. Descend gently for 300 yards (274m), then fork left, remaining on the track to a gate opening and field. Keep straight on to **Bow Creek**, turning left along the water's edge to a stile.

Walk along the foreshore for 110 yards (100m), then bear left as the path rises up through trees and enters a field. Follow this delightful path parallel to Bow Creek, passing the ruins of a lime kiln, and shortly cross a stile to a meadow and footbridge near the creek edge. Head inland for a few yards, then beyond the old quarry and derelict lime kiln, cross a stile and turn immediately right to resume the route alongside the creek.

Leave by a kissing gate to eventually emerge on to a metalled lane in the hamlet of **Tuckenhay**. Turn left, passing the road to a small housing estate, and join a stony track. Ignore arrowed footpath left, then keep right at junction of tracks and gently descend to a lane. Turn left, climb uphill past **Tuckenhay Mill** and soon ascend steeply up a stony track, which shortly becomes a hedged green lane leading to a road by Edgecombe Barn. Turn right, then in 80 yards (73m) bear left along a no through road. On reaching a thatched cottage, take the waymarked footpath left through a gate beside a garage, and follow a grass-centred track gently uphill to pass a series of farm buildings.

Beyond the concrete hardstanding climb a grassy path to a waymarked gate, keep left along the field edge following yellow-arrowed marker posts to a stile in the field corner. Cross a brook and further stile, then proceed along a line of trees to a marker post. Turn right uphill, keeping left of a hedge, climb a stile and shortly reach a driveway and lane.

Turn left along the lane, then in 70 yards (64m) bear right at a fork, signposted 'Cornworthy'. Keep straight ahead on reaching a crossroads and descend into

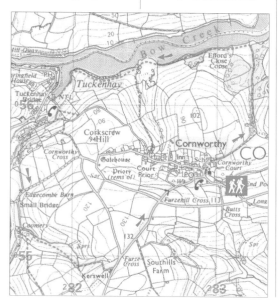

Cornworthy, passing the Old Rectory on your left opposite the church.

POINTS OF INTEREST

Bow Creek

This tranquil tributary of the River Dart once had 15 lime-burning kilns around its edges. Lime was first quarried in the area during the 15th century and used for mortar, but between the 16th and 18th centuries, when lime was applied to the land to reduce soil acidity, the lime-burning trade flourished here due to the demand from remote farms. Nowadays, the creek is a peaceful haven, rich in birdlife, with mallards, shelducks, oystercatchers and herons feeding on the mudflats at low tide.

Tuckenhay

In 1850 the quays around this now quiet little hamlet once bustled with industrial activity, with boats exporting local rope, cider, paper, roadstone and lime. The former port had warehouses, two paper mills, a cider press and numerous lime-burning kilns, but trade from Tuckenhay ceased when the harbour silted up.

Tuckenhay Mill

This imposing complex of buildings, built in 1859 and with an attractive central clock tower, remained a working paper mill producing quality hand-made paper until it closed in 1970. Since then it has been carefully restored and

Seventeenth-century Hunters Lodge Inn at Cornworthy is at the start of the walk

converted into holiday apartments.

Cornworthy

Set in the folds of rolling hills, the village probably developed from the Augustinian Priory of Nuns that was founded here between 1231 and 1238. All that remains of this building is a solitary gatehouse, which can be seen in a private field west of Court Prior Farm on entering the village. St Peter's Church is mainly 15th century, escaping Victorian restoration, and containing a medieval rood screen and fine box pews.

The English Riviera and The South Hams

Checklist

Leisure Information
Places of Interest
Shopping
The Performing Arts
Sports, Activities and the Outdoors
Annual Events and Customs

Leisure Information

TOURIST INFORMATION CENTRES

Brixham
The Old Market House, The Quay. Tel: 01803 852861.
Dartmouth
The Newcomen Engine House, Mayor's Avenue. Tel: 01803 834224.
Dawlish
The Lawn. Tel: 01626 215665.
Kingsbridge
The Quay. Tel: 01548 853195.
Paignton
The Esplanade. Tel: 01803 558383.
Salcombe
Council Hall, Market Street. Tel: 01548 843927.
Teignmouth
The Den. Tel: 01626 215666.
Torquay
Vaughan Parade. Tel: 01803 296296.
Totnes
The Town Mill, Coronation Road. Tel: 01803 863168.

OTHER INFORMATION

Devon Wildlife Trust
Shirehampton House, 35–37 St David's Hill, Exeter. Tel: 01392 279244.
English Heritage
29 Queen Square, Bristol.

Tel: 0117 975 0700
www.english-heritage.org.uk
English Nature Devonteam
Level 2 Renslade House, Bonhay Road, Exeter.
Tel: 01392 88970.
Forest Enterprise England
340 Bristol Business Park, Coldharbour Lane, Bristol. Tel: 0117 906 6000.
National Trust for Devon
Killerton House, Broadclyst, Exeter. Tel: 01392 881691.
www.nationaltrust.org.uk
Parking
Weekly parking tickets are available for Torquay, Paignton and Brixham from Torquay Tourist Information Centre. For the South Hams contact Totnes Tourist Information Centre.
South West Lakes Trust
Highercombe Park, Lewdown, Okehampton. Tel: 01837 871565.

ORDNANCE SURVEY MAPS

Explorer 1:25,000. Sheet 110 (31). Landranger 1:50,000. Sheets 192, 202. Outdoor Leisure 1:25,000. Sheet 20.

Places of Interest

Unless otherwise stated, there will be an admission charge to the following places of interest.

Babbacombe Model Village
Hampton Avenue, Babbacombe. Tel: 01803 315315. Open all year, daily.
Berry Pomeroy Castle
Totnes. Tel: 01803 866618. Open Apr–Oct, daily.
Bowden House Ghostly Tales and Photographic Museum
Totnes. Tel: 01803 863664. Open end May–Sep, most days.
Bradley Manor
Newton Abbot. Open early Apr–Sep, Wed and Thu pm.
Britannia Royal Naval College
Dartmouth. Tel: 01803 834224. Open Etr–Oct.
Brixham Museum
Bolton Cross, Brixham. Tel: 01803 856267. Open Easter–Oct, most days.
'Bygones'
Fore Street, St Marychurch, Torquay. Tel: 01803 326108. Open all year, daily, except Christmas Day.
Cockington Country Park
Torquay. Tel: 01803 606035.
Compton Castle
Compton. Tel: 01803 875740. Open Apr–Oct, certain days.
Cookworthy Museum of Rural Life
The Old Grammar School, 108 Fore Street, Kingsbridge.

Tel: 01548 853235. Open end
Mar–Oct, most days.
Dartmouth Castle
Dartmouth. Tel: 01803 833588.
Open Apr–Oct, daily. Limited
opening Nov–Mar,
Dartmouth Museum
6 Butterwalk, Dartmouth.
Tel: 01803 832923. Open all
year, most days.
Guildhall
Rampart Walk, off High Street,
Totnes. Tel: 01803 862147.
Open Apr–Oct, most days.
**Hedgehog Hospital at
Prickly Ball Farm**
Denbury Road, near Newton
Abbot. Tel: 01626 362319.
Open Mar–Sep, daily.
Kents Cavern Showcaves
The Caves, Wellwood, Torquay.
Tel: 01803 215136. Open all
year, daily; phone for winter
opening.
Newcomen Memorial Engine
The Engine House, Mayors
Avenue, Dartmouth. Tel: 01803
834224. Open all year, most
days.
**Overbecks Museum and
Garden**
Sharpitor. Tel 01548 842893.
Open Museum Apr–Oct most
days, gardens all year, daily.
Paignton Zoo
Totnes Road, Paignton. Tel:
01803 697500. Open all year,
except 25 Dec.
**Paignton and Dartmouth
Steam Railway**
Queens Park Station, Torbay
Road, Paignton. Tel: 01803
555872. Open Jun-Sep, daily;
some days Oct–Nov, Mar–May.
Salcombe Maritime Museum
Market Street. Open Easter–Oct,
daily.
Shaldon Wildlife Trust
Ness Drive, Shaldon. Tel: 01626
872234. Open all year, daily.
**Start Point Lighthouse
Tours**
Start Point.
Tel: 01803 770606.
Torquay Museum
529 Babbacombe Road,
Torquay. Tel: 01803 293975.
**Torre Abbey Historic House
and Gallery**
The Kings Drive, Torquay.
Tel: 01803 293593. Open
Aprr–Oct, daily.

Totnes Castle
Totnes. Tel: 01803 864406.
Open Apr–Oct daily, limited
opening Nov–Mar.
Totnes Elizabethan Museum
70 Fore Street, Totnes.
Tel: 01803 863821. Open
Apr–Oct, most days.
Tuckers Maltings
Teign Road, Osborne Park,
Newton Abbot. Tel: 01626
334734. Open Easter–Oct, most
days.

SPECIAL INTEREST FOR CHILDREN

The following places may be of
interest to visitors with children.
Unless otherwise stated, there
will be an admission charge.
**Adventure Farm Sorley
Tunnel**
Loddiswell Road, Kingsbridge.
Tel: 01548 857711/854078.
Open Apr–Oct, daily.
Babbacombe Model Village
Hampton Avenue, Babbacombe.
Tel: 01803 328669. Open all
year daily, except Christmas
Day.
**Gorse Blossom Miniature
Railway and Woodland Park**
Liverton, Newton Abbot. Tel:
01626 821361. Open end
May–early Sep. Phone for other
times.
Woodland Leisure Park
Blackawton, near Dartmouth.
Tel: 01803 712598. Open all
year daily, mid-Mar to early Nov;
telephone for winter opening
times.

Shopping

Brixham
Pannier Market, Scala Hall, Tue
and Fri.
Dartmouth
Main shopping area Duke Street.
Market Fri.
Dawlish Warren
Market Tue mid-May to end
Sep.
Kingsbridge
Market, The Quay, Tue and Thu.
Newton Abbot
Trago Mills Shopping and
Leisure Centre, Stover, near
Newton Abbot.
Livestock Market, Wed. Outdoor
Market, Market Square, Sat.

Torquay
Fleet Walk, Pavilion Shopping
Centre. Indoor Market, Market
Street, all year Mon–Sat. Market
at Torquay Ring Road (Gallows
Gate), Mon, mid-May to end
Sep. Flea Market, Town Hall,
Thu.
Totnes
Elizabethan Market, May–Sep,
Tue. Totnes Civic Hall, Fri and
Sat. Also antiques, crafts and flea
markets.

LOCAL SPECIALITIES

Clotted Cream
Shops will send cream by post.
Craft Centres
Dartington Cider Press Centre,
at Shinners Bridge, Totnes.
Tel: 01803 864171. Higher
Street Gallery, Higher Street,
Dartmouth. Tel: 01803 833157.
Pottery
Cockington Court Craft Studios,
Cockington. Tel: 01803 606035.
Dartmouth Pottery, Warfleet
Creek. Tel: 01803 832258.
Simon Drew Gallery, Foss Street,
Dartmouth. Tel: 01803 832832.
Wine
Sharpham Vineyard,
Ashprington, Totnes. Tel: 01803
732203.

The Performing Arts

Babbacombe Theatre
Babbacombe Downs. Torquay.
Tel: 01803 328385.
Brixham Theatre
New Road, Brixham. Tel: 01803
858338.

The Ship Inn, Newton Abbot

Dartington Arts
The Gallery, Dartington Hall, Totnes. Tel: 01803 847070.
Little Theatre
5 Marks Road, Torquay.
Tel: 01803 299330.
Palace Avenue Theatre
Palace Avenue, Paignton.
Tel: 01803 665800.
Princess Theatre
Torbay Road, Torquay.
Tel: 08702 414120.

Sports, Activities and the Outdoors

ANGLING

Sea
For information about trips in the area contact the local tourist information centres.
Fly
Newhouse Fishery, Newhouse Farm, Moreleigh, Totnes.
Tel: 01548 821426.
Coarse
Combe Fishery, Coombe Farm, Kingsbridge. Tel: 01548 852038.

BEACHES AND COVES

In and around Brixham
Breakwater Beach (EC Blue Flag). Churston Cove. Fishcombe. Shoalstone, with open-air seawater swimming pool. St Mary's Bay, long, mostly sandy beach.
In and around Dartmouth
Blackpool Sands (EC Blue Flag), no dogs during main season. Strete Gate (EC Blue Flag). Slapton Sands. Torcross.
In and around Dawlish
Boat Cove. Coryton Cove. Dawlish Warren (EC Blue Flag). Shell Cove.
In and around Paignton
Broadsands Beach. Elberry Cove. Fairy Cove. Goodrington Sands. Paignton Sands. Preston Sands. Saltern Cove.
In and around Salcombe
North Sands. Millbay, Sunny Cove. South Sands.
In and around Teignmouth
Herring Cove. Mackerel Cove. Ness Cove. Teignmouth Beach.
In and around Torquay
Ansteys Cove. Babbacombe. Corbyn Sands. Livermead. Maidencombe. Meadfoot Beach,

EC Blue Flag. Oddicombe, EC Blue Flag. Preston Sands. Torre Abbey Sands. Watcombe.

BOAT TRIPS

Sailings on the River Dart between Dartmouth and Totnes. Details from Riverlink, 5 Lower Street, Dartmouth. Tel: 01803 832109.
Dartmouth
Dartmouth Boat Hire Centre, North Embankment. Tel: 01803 722367.
Greenway
Self Drive Motor Boats, Greenway Quay, near Churston. Tel: 01803 844010.

COUNTRY PARKS AND NATURE RESERVES

Berry Head Country Park.
Tel: 01803 882619.
Dawlish Warren Nature Reserve Visitor Centre. Tel: 01626 863980.
Slapton Ley. Guided walks in July and August. Tel: 01548 580466.

CYCLE HIRE

Teignmouth
Mylor Cycles, 10 Northumberland Place.
Tel: 01626 778460.
Torquay
Simply The Bike, 100–102 Belgrave Road. Tel: 01803 200024.

GOLF COURSES

Bigbury on Sea
Bigbury Golf Club. Tel: 01548 810557.
Dawlish Warren
The Warren Golf Club.
Tel: 01626 862255.
Newton Abbot
Stover Golf Club, Bovey Road.
Tel: 01626 352460.
Teignmouth
Teignmouth Golf Club, Haldon Moor. Tel: 01626 777070.
Torquay
Torquay Golf Course, Petitor Road.
Tel: 01803 314591.

HORSE-RIDING

Cockington
Cockington Riding Stables, Cockington Village. Tel: 01803 606860.

Kingsbridge
Sorley Tunnel Riding School, Loddiswell. Tel: 01548 856662.
Newton Abbot
Honeysuckle Farm Equestrian Centre, Haccombe with Coombe. Tel: 01626 355944.

SAILING

Dartmouth
Dittisham Sailing School. Tel: 01803 883716.
Salcombe
The Island Cruising Club, 10 Island Street. Tel: 01548 843481.
Teignmouth
Teign Corinthian Yacht Club, Eastcliff Country Park, Dawlish Road. Tel: 01626 772734 (am).
Torquay
International Sailing School, Beacon Quay, Torquay. Tel: 01803 291849.
Jib Set Marine, Beacon Quay, Torquay. Tel: 01803 295414.

Annual Events and Customs

Brixham
Heritage Festival, early June. International Trawler Race, late June.
Mardi Gras, late July.
Dartmouth
Music Festival, mid-May. Carnival, late June/early July. Regatta, late August.
Dawlish
Carnival, mid-August.
Folk Festival, early September.
Kingsbridge
Fair Week, mid-July. Agricultural Show, early September. Extravaganza and Illuminated Winter Carnival, late November.

The checklists give details of just some of the facilities within the area covered by this guide. Further information can be obtained from Tourist Information Centres.

Exeter and East Devon

This quiet corner of Devon is a delight to explore because, although it is one of the most accessible from the rest of England, bisected by both the M5 and the A30, it has retained much of its old world character. Its countryside of rolling pastures and river valleys is dotted with unspoilt villages and even its resorts – Seaton, Sidmouth, Budleigh Salterton and Exmouth – preserve the quiet dignity of their Regency and Victorian heyday. Exeter, on the other hand, is an attractive and fascinating city, balancing its long and important history with the needs of its lively modern community.

AXMINSTER   Map ref SX2998

The name of this pleasant Devon town is inextricably linked with the world-famous carpets which are still produced here. The industry was originated in 1755 by Thomas Whitty, whose factory produced many custom-made carpets of the highest quality for some of Britain's greatest mansions and palaces. Sadly, the popular factory tours have been stopped by new safety regulations.

Apart from its carpets, Axminster is a busy market town with a cluster of attractive streets around the central Trinity Square (actually a triangle), which is

THE LARGEST FIREPLACE IN THE WORLD
Shute Barton Manor claims to have the largest fireplace in England, and possibly in the world. The cavernous stone structure stretches for 22 feet (6.6m) across the entrance hall and stands 7 feet (2.1m) high.

The big church of St Nicholas, Axminster, dominates the town square

DEVON COB

Many of Devon's prettiest old cottages are built of cob, a traditional building material of the county. It is basically clay, but with a variety of other materials such as straw, sheep's wool, horsehair – even manure. The materials have to be kneaded together with water to get the right consistency for building, and traditionally this was done by placing them in the cattle sheds, where the animals' feet would do the hard work. With its muddy appearance, cob walls would seem to be susceptible to rain damage, but are surprisingly resilient to the elements and this method of building is enjoying a modest revival within the county.

On Hawksdown Hill, high above the pretty harbour at Axmouth, is the site of an Iron-Age hillfort

dominated by the large church. Near by, the Old Court House in Church Street houses the town's information centre and behind it is a delightful courtyard garden.

Just to the southwest of Axminster, tucked away in the country lanes south of the A35 Honiton road, is Shute Barton Manor (National Trust). This delightful old house with battlemented turrets dates from about 1380 and is one of the most important surviving non-fortified manor houses in the country. Shute Barton has been occupied by the Carew Pole family since the 16th century and their presence accounts for much of the charm, with family paraphernalia such as fishing rods, Wellington boots and their grandchildren's toys; the family dogs may well greet you in the entrance hall.

AXMOUTH Map ref SY2591

Axmouth is not only very pretty, it has been here a very long time. The Roman Fosse Way crossed the wide River Axe here, and by the 7th century the settlement was well established. Today it presents a picturesque scene of colour-washed thatched cottages grouped around St Michael's Church, which dates back to Norman times. The village was once an important port, but as the river silted up, the size of vessels able to navigate it reduced until it could only accommodate yachts and pleasure craft. Today it is popular not only with weekend sailors, but also with windsurfers and birdwatchers, and a lovely walk alongside the estuary gives access to the Axmouth-Lyme Regis undercliffs.

BEER Map ref SY2289

The lovely little fishing village of Beer is in one of the most sheltered positions along this coast and its fishermen gained a reputation for hardy seamanship because they could put to sea when others were kept at home by the pounding waves. Beer is not only noted for its fishermen, it also has the most westerly chalk cliffs in England, contrasting vividly with the deep red cliffs near by and the lush green of the surrounding countryside (see Walk on page 108). It once had a renowned lace-making industry, established here by refugees from The Netherlands, and the quality of the work rivalled the more famous Honiton lace. Beer lace was used to decorate Queen Victoria's wedding dress.

To the west of the village are Pecorama Pleasure Gardens, set high on a hillside overlooking the village and the coastline. Apart from the beautiful gardens, there is a miniature steam and diesel passenger railway which offers some of the best views across Lyme Bay, and an exhibition of railway modelling.

The Beer Quarry Caves offer a totally different experience, with an hour-long tour of these man-made caverns which extend for a quarter of a mile (0.4km) in each direction. The Romans worked the quarries nearly 2,000 years ago, and the vast caverns with vaulted roofs and natural stone pillars were hewn by hand over the intervening centuries. The Cretaceous limestone which was quarried at Beer was prized by stone masons because it is soft and easy to carve when it first comes out of the ground, but hardens when it is exposed to the elements. Creamy-white in colour and smooth in texture, it provides a perfect medium for their craft, which can be seen to its best advantage in Exeter Cathedral.

Traditional wooden beach huts line the shingle at Beer

A SMUGGLER'S TALE
Jack Rattenbury, born in Beer in 1778, was Devon's most notorious smuggler. Disillusioned by the life of a fisherman by the time he was 14, he went to sea as an honest crewman, but his vessel was captured by the French and various escapades took him across the Atlantic and back. After that, life in Beer was dull, and smuggling offered him the excitement he craved and the money he desperately needed. There followed a life of forays across the Channel for contraband, dodging the Excise men (not always successfully), several prison sentences and some daring escapes, but nothing deterred him from his life of crime. His life story was eventually written down by a retired Unitarian minister from Seaton.

THE ROLLE FAMILY

The Bicton estate passed by marriage into the Rolle family in the early 17th century, placing them among the greatest landowners in the country, and by 1706 they were lords of 45 manors. The family was divided by the Civil War, but Sir John Rolle was among those who escorted Charles II on his triumphant return from exile in 1660. In the 18th century Lord John Rolle was a great benefactor both in the locality of Bicton and in his estates in the Bahamas, where he freed all of his slaves and gave them land well before slavery was abolished. Many Bahamians adopted the name of Rolle in honour of his humanitarian action.

The gardens at Bicton Park feature a superb orangery and an ever-changing display

BICTON PARK   Map ref SY0786

The beautiful gardens at Bicton were created in about 1730 to designs by the great André le Nôtre (1613–99), gardener to Louis XIV and the architect of the magnificent gardens at Versailles. Stand in front of the orangery and look down over the three great terraces of lawns, formal flower beds and statues, with a great rectangular pond with its central fountain at the lowest level. From there the eye is drawn up again through a swathe cut through the trees to a distant obelisk. This is the focal point of the 50 acres of Bicton Park, but there are many other delights to explore. Just to one side is the American Garden, with rocky outcrops and some interesting trees from that continent. Here, too, is the Shell House, built of flints but containing a collection of shells from around the world.

The peaceful Oriental Garden has trees and shrubs with oriental connections planted around a summerhouse and little wooden bridges, and towards the other side of the park is the Pinetum, already a fine collection of species, but still developing. There are various glasshouses too, including the Temperate House, Orchid House, Geranium House and Fuchsia House.

One of the best introductions to the park as a whole can be gained from taking a ride on Bicton's narrow-gauge railway, which departs from a station near to the entrance and hauls purpose-built carriages past the lake and through the Pinetum, taking in wonderful views of the Italian Gardens, before making a loop to the Hermitage Garden on the far side of the lake.

Other attractions include an excellent countryside museum with wagons and a cider press among its displays, a wonderful indoor soft-play area for younger children and a good outdoor playground.

BRANSCOMBE Map ref SY1988

Branscombe is gorgeous. It stretches along one of the prettiest combes on the south coast, with picture-book thatched cottages – complete with roses round the door – lovely inns and an ancient church. St Winifred's dates back to just after the Norman Conquest and its tower contains a priest's room, from the time when the priest lived in the church.

Until 1987, the village bakery was the last traditional bakery in use in the county. It, along with the old forge, Manor Mill and some farms and cottages, has now been preserved by the National Trust and visitors can see the large faggot-fired oven, the great dough bins and other traditional baking equipment in the baking room. The rest of the building is used as a tearoom, which is up to the usual standard of the Trust. More of their delicious cakes and cream teas can be enjoyed at the beach, where the wood and thatched tearooms have a lovely outlook, with indoor and outdoor tables.

The drive from the village to the beach is along a narrow lane which goes steeply up and then down again to the sheltered bay, nestling between huge red-coloured cliffs. Much of the land to either side, including farmland and foreshore in places, is in the care of the National Trust and there are lovely walks, including one from the village (see also Walk on page 108). The beach here is shingle, with rock pools to explore at low tide, and is good for swimming.

A delectable corner of Branscombe that is for ever England

THE HOOKEN LANDSLIP

Between Branscombe and Beer is a dramatic piece of coastline, formed when a huge chunk of land broke away from the cliff in the late 18th century. It is now clothed in lush green vegetation, with great white stone turrets, The Pinnacles, protruding skywards, and can be seen as part of our Walk on page 108.

Beer, Hooken Cliffs and Branscombe Vale

A scenic cliff path walk, with two steep ascents, from the small resort of Beer to the picturesque village of Branscombe. With so much to interest the lingering walker this walk could easily make a whole day out.

Time: 2½–3hours. Distance: 5 miles (8km).
Location: 1 mile (1.6km) west of Seaton.
Start: Cliff car park on Common Lane, Beer.
(OS grid ref: SY227888.)
OS Maps: Explorer 116 (Lyme Regis & Bridport)
1:25,000.
Explorer 115 (Exmouth & Sidmouth) 1:25,000 is required for the diversion to Branscombe church.
See Key for Walks on page 121.

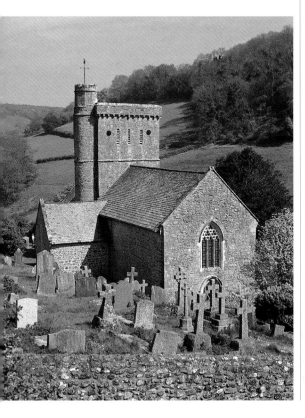

ROUTE DIRECTIONS

Take the arrowed coast path 'Branscombe Mouth' along Little Lane, near the car park exit. Shortly, bear left in front of a caravan site to a wooden swing gate. Proceed on the defined path through a field to a another swing gate, then keep close to the fenced cliff edge, following the gently rising waymarked path via gates around **Beer Head**.

Before reaching the cliff-top building/lookout, climb the arrowed stile and descend steeply into **Hooken Undercliff**. Keep to the path through this spectacular landslip area, eventually merging with a track that passes through a caravan site. Go through a gate beside a cattle grid and bear diagonally left downhill on a worn path to a kissing gate and Branscombe Mouth.

Bear left with coast path sign, cross the footbridge by the ford and follow the drive in front of the Sea Shanty café. Turn right along the valley bottom path beside the café and car park. Shortly, go through a gate and cross a footbridge over a stream. Beyond a further small gate follow the path along the meadow edge to a gate and footbridge in the field corner.

To visit the working Smithy (NT), the Old Bakery Tea

St Winifred's Church at Branscombe

Room and **Branscombe** church, keep ahead through the meadow to a stile, continue on a metalled lane to the main village road and turn left. Return to the footbridge and turn right to a gate to join the lane beside the brook for the village centre.

To continue on the main walk, bear left to a gate and follow the lane into the village. On reaching a junction turn sharp right uphill then turn left along a narrow lane, and in 30 yards (27m) take the arrowed path right to begin a steep ascent up Stockham Hill (NT). Cross a stile, keep left along the fence, then ignore a stile on your left and continue uphill, signposted 'Beer'. In 200 yards (183m), by another stile, bear right to reach a stile on the woodland fringe.

Keep left along the field edge, then at a junction of paths take the route arrowed 'Mare Lane' to a stile. Cross an open field on to another stile, then proceed ahead along a track, which gradually descends towards Beer. In half a mile (0.8km) pass between a car park and **Pecorama** to

a T-junction.

Turn left, then as the road bears left downhill, take the narrow waymarked path right between houses. Shortly, cross a road, then cross a second road on to a driveway, soon to follow a defined path which cuts across the top of the town, eventually reaching Common Lane just below the cliff car park.

POINTS OF INTEREST

Beer and Beer Head
This attractive little resort and fishing village with quaint narrow streets was once the haunt of smugglers. Stone has been quarried here since Roman times and Beer stone was used to build Exeter Cathedral. Beer Head, a magnificent chalk promontory rising 426 feet (130m) above the sea, has splendid views east to Portland and west to Start Point.

Hooken Undercliff
A dramatic 10-acre landslip

broke away from the cliff in 1790, creating a wilderness of columns and pinnacles. Thick undergrowth provides a haven for many species of birds.

Branscombe
A delightful village of cob and thatch cottages scattered on the steep wooded slopes of a combe. In the upper village are a working thatched Smithy (NT) and the old village bakery (now a museum and tea room). The ancient Church of St Winifred has a Norman tower and nave, an unusual 18th-century three-decker pulpit and fragments of medieval wall paintings.

Pecorama Pleasure Gardens
The miniature steam and diesel railway enjoys views across Lyme Bay as it runs through the Pleasure Gardens, where attractions include an exhibition of railway modelling, an aviary and children's activity area.

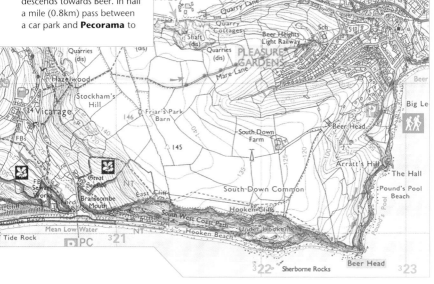

The curving beach at Budleigh leads irresistably to the cliffs at the end

The Octagon, next door to the museum, is where Millais stayed while he was engaged upon his famous painting *The Boyhood of Raleigh*, now in The Tate Gallery in London (Raleigh was born a short distance inland at Hayes Barton). Another notable resident was General Simcoe (1756–1806), the first Governor of Upper Canada, who lived in Fore Street Hill in the house now known as 'Little Hill'.

BUDLEIGH SALTERTON Map ref SY0682

Budleigh Salterton became a resort in the wake of royal visits to nearby Sidmouth in Georgian and Victorian times, but it was – and remains – a quiet place, free of much of the bustle and amusements often associated with seaside holidays. It lies on the western side of the Otter estuary (it was originally called Ottermouth) where one of its main industries used to be salt-panning, hence the 'Salterton' part of the name. The beach, overlooked from the west by high red cliffs, is all pebbles, which shelve quite steeply into the sea, but swimming is safe enough in calm weather. If you want some sand, walk westwards along the coast path to Littleham Cove – small, remote and very sheltered.

Many fine old buildings remain in the town, including Fairlynch, now a small but interesting museum which has displays on local history, the natural history of the River Otter and the Budleigh Salterton Railway, as well as a beautiful display of Devon lace. The museum also has a fine costume collection.

A little way inland is Otterton, a particularly pretty village of thatched cottages. The watermill here is the last working mill on the River Otter and visitors can see it in operation – milling is done about three days a week, but the wheel and machinery turns every day. There are various displays on milling, craft workshops, a craft shop, a bookshop and art gallery and an exhibition on east Devon lace.

EXETER Map ref SX9292

To many people Exeter is the place at the end of the M5, which you go past on your way to the holiday resorts of south Devon and Cornwall. Anyone who doesn't take the time to stop and explore this remarkable city is missing a real treat because it has just about everything you could wish for – a long and important history, magnificent old buildings, fascinating places to visit, a good shopping centre, a lively arts programme and one or two surprises – where else, for instance, can you explore the tunnels of a medieval water supply?

At its heart is the spectacular cathedral which rises up from spacious lawns so that the whole building can be seen in all its glory. The earliest part, the two great towers, date from 1110, but most of the building is of the 14th century, including the beautiful West Front, with its medieval figures of apostles, prophets and soldiers. Inside the cathedral are treasures too numerous to mention in detail, but the first thing to catch the eye (and to hold it) is the roof of the central aisle. This is the longest unbroken Gothic vault in the world, dating from 1369 – magnifying mirrors on wheels help you to study these without getting a crick in your neck.

In the centre of the cathedral is the choir with magnificent oak carving. The Bishop's Throne, dating from 1312, is undoubtedly the finest in the country, and the 49 canopied stalls, dating from the 19th century, reflect its style. Magnificently decorated tombs and monuments, delightful features among the carvings and peaceful little chapels make the cathedral a place where you can spend as much time as you have available.

On a nice day, the Cathedral Close is a lovely place to linger, to sit on the grass or the low wall which surrounds it and soak up the atmosphere, but if your time is limited, don't sit for too long because there is so much more to see. One of the city's other major attractions is the revitalised historic Quayside, where it is easy to imagine wool trading vessels of yesteryear

CURIOUS CARVINGS
Though the stalls in the choir of Exeter Cathedral are of relatively recent date, they incorporate the oldest complete set of medieval misericords in the country. The occupants of the stalls were required to stand throughout services, but could fold down a little hinged 'seat' to give them a little respite. Beneath each of these is a medieval carving (misericord) – look out for the elephant, which is thought to be styled on the first elephant ever to be brought to England (in 1253). St James's Chapel also has some unusual carvings in stone – of the cathedral's cat, a mouse and a rugby player.

The West Front of Exeter Cathedral is not to be missed; miraculously, the cathedral survived unscathed the bombing of the city centre in 1942

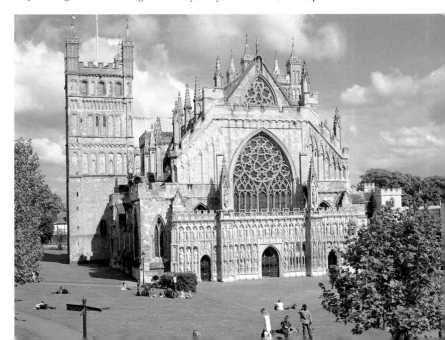

*Cathedral Close in the
historic city of Exeter*

UNDERGROUND PASSAGES
Exeter's network of
underground passages which
brought water to the
medieval city can be
explored; the entrance is
under the Princesshay
shopping precinct. Visitors
must be fit and healthy, and
definitely not inclined to
claustrophobia! Flat shoes are
essential.

BUDLEIGH SALTERTON   Map ref SY0682

Budleigh Salterton became a resort in the wake of royal
visits to nearby Sidmouth in Georgian and Victorian
times, but it was – and remains – a quiet place, free of
much of the bustle and amusements often associated
with seaside holidays. It lies on the western side of the
Otter estuary (it was originally called Ottermouth) where
one of its main industries used to be salt-panning, hence
the 'Salterton' part of the name. The beach, overlooked
from the west by high red cliffs, is all pebbles, which
shelve quite steeply into the sea, but swimming is safe
enough in calm weather. If you want some sand, walk
westwards along the coast path to Littleham Cove –
small, remote and very sheltered.

Many fine old buildings remain in the town, including
Fairlynch, now a small but interesting museum which
has displays on local history, the natural history of the
River Otter and the Budleigh Salterton Railway, as well as
a beautiful display of Devon lace. The museum also has a
fine costume collection.

A little way inland is Otterton, a particularly pretty
village of thatched cottages. The watermill here is the
last working mill on the River Otter and visitors can see
it in operation – milling is done about three days a week,
but the wheel and machinery turns every day. There are
various displays on milling, craft workshops, a craft
shop, a bookshop and art gallery and an exhibition on
east Devon lace.

EXETER   Map ref SX9292

To many people Exeter is the place at the end of the M5,
which you go past on your way to the holiday resorts of
south Devon and Cornwall. Anyone who doesn't take

housing complex, the latter enjoying superb sea views.

As a resort, Exmouth began to develop at the end of the 18th century and today it is a pleasant town and popular resort, with long sandy beaches where there are rock pools to explore at half-tide.

Two miles (3.2km) north is A La Ronde (National Trust), a 16-sided thatched house built in 1796 for two spinster cousins, Jane and Mary Parminter. Both the house and its contents are the result of their Grand Tour of Europe and the interiors are the result of their own particular eccentricities. The rooms are arranged around an octagonal hall, and the Shell Gallery is decorated with a collage of shells, feathers and other natural materials.

HONITON   Map ref ST1600

This is a town which is easy to explore because just about everything is in the High Street, a charming wide thoroughfare lined with Georgian buildings. Its unity of style is due to a series of fires during the 18th century, which destroyed much of the original town that had stood here since about 1200. The straightness of its main street is due to the fact that the town was originally built astride an old Roman road.

High Street is one of those streets that just begs you to get out of your car and wander up and down for a while, to browse around the variety of little shops, many of them selling antiques, and explore the little courtyards and alleyways that run off at right angles. The old Pannier Market, where goods were once brought from the surrounding area for sale, has now been converted into an attractive little parade of shops.

Of course, what Honiton is most famous for is lace, and there is a wonderful collection in the Allhallows Museum, housed in Honiton's oldest building, a 13th-century chapel beside St Paul's Church. The museum also has lace-making demonstrations and displays which relate to the town's pottery and clock-making industries.

HONITON LACE

Honiton lace consists of small motifs which are then attached to sheer net – even the net was hand made until the early 19th century. The craft originated when Flemish refugees came to the area in the early 16th century, and by the 17th century it was so highly prized that it was used as currency during the Jacobite rebellion. In 1840 100 workers produced the lace for Queen Victoria's wedding dress – at a cost of £1,000. More recently, a Honiton lace-maker was commissioned to produce a new jabot for the Speaker of the House of Commons. There were 3,600 lace-makers in the Honiton area in the early 1700s, but it is no longer produced commercially.

The extensive formal gardens and landscaping are a year-round delight at Killerton

THE BEAR'S HUT AND THE ICE HOUSE
Close to the rock garden at Killerton is a strange little house which was built in 1808. In the 1860s it became home to a pet black bear which had been brought back from Canada by Gilbert Acland. Near by is the ice house, built at around the same time, which could hold 40 tons of ice for use in the kitchen. It took 30 men five days to fill it.

KILLERTON HOUSE AND GARDENS
Map ref SS9700

Killerton House was built in 1778–9 for Sir Thomas Acland and remained the family home until it was given to the National Trust in 1944. While it has never been hailed as an architectural triumph, it is not unattractive, particularly in its beautiful garden setting, and it is a fascinating house to visit, chiefly because of the imaginative displays of its famous costume collection. Over 4,000 items of 18th- and 19th-century costume were accumulated by Paulise de Bush during World War II and some 40 original dresses at a time are displayed in appropriate room settings; these are changed annually.

The 18 acres of landscaped gardens are the real glory of Killerton, with rare trees, shrub borders, sweeping lawns and planted beds, beyond which stretch the open park and woodland. There is a delightful rock garden, and in Killerton Clump are traces of Iron-Age earthworks. Special events at Killerton include guided walks around the gardens, gardening talks and demonstrations, theatre and charity events.

OTTERY ST MARY   Map ref SX1095

This pleasant little town lies on the River Otter and was the birthplace in 1772 of the poet Samuel Taylor Coleridge, whose father was vicar of St Mary's Church. The church may seem too grand for a sleepy little Devon town, and it certainly had more modest beginnings in the 13th century, but in 1340 Bishop John de Grandisson had it enlarged, with Exeter Cathedral much in his mind. The interior is rich in medieval craftsmanship and there is an ancient astronomical clock which is still in working order.

Not far away from Ottery is Cadhay, a classic Tudor manor house which was enlarged and remodelled in

Georgian style. It is an interesting house with a history of extreme ups and downs – one minute a social honeypot, the next declining as the owners fell into debt after supporting the wrong side in the Civil War. A new owner in the 18th century raised its status once more, only for it to become a kind of boarding house for agricultural workers in the 19th century. But in 1909 Cadhay was rescued and restored and is now a fascinating and charming place to visit.

SEATON   Map ref SY2490

If you start at the Devon/Dorset border, Seaton is the first of a series of sedate resorts that stretch along this part of the coast, but was the last to give itself up to the holiday market. Not until the late 19th century did it start to expand and provide for the seaside holiday market. It lies on the west side of the estuary of the River Axe and its wide, sloping shingle beach is backed by a mixture of Victorian and more modern buildings.

One great attraction is the Seaton Tramway with its scenic route along the River Axe as far as Colyton. Taking 25 minutes each way, the journey is by open-topped double-decker trams (or closed-in single-decker in winter) and gives wonderful views and the opportunity to spot some of the abundant birdlife along the river, including swans, shelduck, oystercatchers and grey heron. Colyton, at the other end of the track, is an attractive and historic town well worth exploring.

SIDMOUTH   Map ref SY1287

This is a quiet and genteel resort, and has been since it was favoured by royal patronage in the early 19th century. Much of its architecture goes back to Regency days, with elegant wrought-iron balconies and white-painted façades, and colourful gardens and floral displays enhance the scene. One of these Regency buildings, in

A GARDENER'S DELIGHT
One of the main attractions of Ottery St Mary is the Otter Nurseries, one of the biggest garden centres in the country, which has vast displays of plants and a peaceful koi carp pool as well as all the usual plants, greenhouses, fish and ponds and garden furniture for sale.

Approach Sidmouth from the east on a minor road and you will pass through the old ford

Sidmouth's wide Esplanade fills with musicians and dancers from all corners of the globe during the summer festival, which culminates in a noisy torchlit procession through the town

SIDMOUTH INTERNATIONAL FOLK FESTIVAL
A complete transformation comes over (or overcomes) Sidmouth during the first week in August, when singers, dancers and musicians from all over the world, and their following of 'folkies', descend on the town for its famous festival. About 500 organised events are staged at various venues around the town, not to mention the impromptu ones that occur whenever two or more performers find themselves in any previously peaceful pub, street corner, park or bit of beach.

Church Street, houses the Sid Vale Heritage Centre with interesting collections and local history; guided walks depart from here two mornings a week. Visitors with a scientific bent should check out the Norman Lockyer Observatory on Salcombe Hill, with its planetarium, radio and weather stations, and historic telescopes.

Sidmouth was quick to grasp the possibilities of the seaside holiday industry, and became particularly popular after the visit in 1819 of the Duke of Kent and his daughter, later Queen Victoria, but the town can't be said to have sold out to more modern holiday attractions. It was ever a dignified resort, and remains aloof from the noisy nightlife and amusement arcades that invaded many of its counterparts.

UFFCULME Map ref ST0612
This charming little village in the valley of the River Culm was once an important wool centre. Coldharbour Mill is now a working wool museum with its original wool-making machinery, 18-foot (5.5m) waterwheel and a 1910 steam engine – a Pollit and Wigzell drop valve, horizontal, cross-compound engine, for those who know about this kind of thing. For nearly 200 years wool and worsted yarn has been produced here and visitors are able to see all stages of production, with guides along the way to explain what is going on.

Also on display at the mill is the New World Tapestry, one of the largest embroideries in the world, which is a 264-feet (80-m) long illustration in stitches of the English colonisation of the Americas between 1583 and 1642. After the tour you can walk by the mill stream, picnic by the pond or visit the shop.

Exeter and East Devon

Leisure Information

Places of Interest

Shopping

The Performing Arts

Sports, Activities and the Outdoors

Annual Events and Customs

Checklist

Leisure Information

TOURIST INFORMATION CENTRES

Axminster
The Old Courthouse, Church Street. Tel: 01297 34386.
Budleigh Salterton
Fore Street.
Tel: 01395 445275.
Exeter
Civic Centre, Paris Street. Tel: 01392 265700.
Exmouth
Alexandra Terrace. Tel: 01395 222299.
Honiton
Dowell Street East Car Park. Tel: 01404 43716.
Ottery St Mary
Tel: 01404 813964.
Sidmouth
Ham Lane. Tel: 01395 516441.

OTHER INFORMATION

Devon Wildlife Trust
Shirehampton House, 35–37 St David's Hill, Exeter. Tel: 01392 279244.
English Heritage
29 Queen Square, Bristol.
Tel: 0117 975 0700
www.english-heritage.org.uk
English Nature Devonteam
Level 2 Renslade House, Bonhay

Road, Exeter. Tel: 01392 88970.
Forest Enterprise England
340 Bristol Business Park, Coldharbour Lane, Bristol. Tel: 0117 906 6000.
National Trust for Devon
Killerton House, Broadclyst, Exeter. Tel: 01392 881691.
www.nationaltrust.org.uk
Parking
Parking permits covering Axminster, Budleigh Salterton, Beer, Colyton and Seaton, Honiton, Exmouth and Lympstone, Sidmouth and Ottery St Mary are available from East Devon District Council or Sidmouth Tourist Information Centre.
South West Lakes Trust
Highercombe Park, Lewdown, Okehampton. Tel: 01837 871565.

ORDNANCE SURVEY MAPS

Explorer 1:25,000. Sheets 115 (30), 116 (29).
Landranger 1:50,000. Sheets 192, 193.

Places of Interest

Unless otherwise stated, there will be an admission charge to the following places of interest.

A La Ronde
Summer Lane, Exmouth.
Tel: 01395 265514. Open Apr–Oct, most days.
Allhallows Museum
High Street , Honiton. Tel: 01404 44966. Open Apr–Oct, daily except Sun.
Beer Quarry Caves
Quarry Lane, Beer. Tel: 01297 680282. Open early Apr–Oct, daily.
Bicton Park Gardens
East Budleigh. Tel: 01395 568465. Open all year, daily except 25 Dec.
Cadhay
Ottery St Mary. Tel: 01404 812432. Limited opening.
Coldharbour Mill Working Wool Museum
Coldharbour Mill, Uffculme.
Tel: 01884 840960. Open Apr–Oct, daily.
Fairlynch Museum
Fore Street, Budleigh Salterton. Open Etr–Oct, daily.
Guildhall
High Street, Exeter.
Tel: 01392 201910. Open when not in use. Times are posted outside. Free.
Killerton House and Garden
(off B3181). Tel: 01392 881345. Open House: mid-Mar to Oct

most days; gardens: all year daily.

Norman Lockyer Observatory
Salcombe Hill, Sidmouth. Tel: 01395 579941. Open some afternoons in summer and one evening a month throughout the year.

Otterton Mill Centre
Otterton. Tel: 01395 568521. Open all year, daily.

Powderham Castle
Powderham. Tel: 01626 890243. Open Apr–Oct, daily except Sat.

Quay House Visitor Centre
Exeter. Tel: 01392 265213. Open Etr–Oct, daily.

Royal Albert Memorial Museum
Queen Street, Exeter. Tel: 01392 265858. Open all year, most days. Free.

Sid Vale Heritage Centre
Church Street, Sidmouth. Tel: 01395 516139. Open Easter–Oct, most days.

Underground Passages
Boots Arcade, High Street, Exeter. Tel: 01392 265887. Open all year, most days.

SPECIAL INTEREST FOR CHILDREN

The following places may be of interest to visitors with children. Unless otherwise stated, there will be an admission charge.

Adventureland and Family Fun Park
Verbeer Manor, Willand. Tel: 08700 344437. Many attractions. Open Mar–Nov, daily.

Bicton Park Gardens
East Budleigh. Tel: 01395 568465. Open all year daily, except 25 Dec.

Crealy Country
Clyst St Mary, near Exeter. Tel: 01395 233200. Adventure playgrounds, animals etc. Open all year, daily except 24–26 Dec.

Donkey Sanctuary
Sidmouth. Tel 01395 578222. Open all year, daily. Free.

Farway Countryside Park
Farway. Tel: 01404 871367. 108 acres of countryside. Indoor garden with butterflies and birds. Open end Mar–Oct, daily; weekends in winter.

Pecorama
Underleys, Beer. Tel: 01297 21542. Open: early Apr–Sep, most days, phone for winter opening.

Shopping

Axminster
Weekly livestock market.

Beer
Arts and crafts. Exeter Guildhall Shopping Centre (undercover), off High Street/Queen Street. Harlequin off Queen Street/Paul Street.

Exeter
Markets in Sidwell Street/St George's, undercover in Fore Street.

Honiton
High Street.

Sidmouth
Sidmouth Shopping Centre, 91 High Street. Deldefield Antiques Collectors Centre, 15 Fore Street.

LOCAL SPECIALITIES

Cider
Green Valley Cider, Marsh Barton Farm, Clyst St George. Tel: 01392 876658.

Clotted Cream
Available throughout the county. Many shops will despatch cream by post.

Pottery
Ark Pottery, Higher Barnes, Wiggaton, Ottery St Mary. Tel: 01404 812628. Woodbury Pottery, Greenway, Woodbury. Tel: 01395 233475.

Wine
Manstree, Shillingsford St George. Tel: 01392 832218.

Woollens
Coldharbour Mill Working Wool Museum, Uffculme. Tel: 01884 840960.

The Performing Arts

Northcott
Stocker Road, Exeter. Tel: 01392 54853.

Phoenix Centre
Bradninch Place, Gandy Street, Exeter. Tel: 01392 421111.

Westpoint
Clyst St Mary, Exeter. Tel: 01392 444777. Concerts, ice spectaculars, exhibitions.

Sports, Activities and the Outdoors

ANGLING

Sea
For information on trips in the area contact the local tourist information centres.

Fly
Lower Moorhaline Farm, Yarcombe, near Honiton. Tel: 01404 861284. Watercress Farm, Kerswell Springs, Chudleigh. Tel: 01626 852168.

Coarse
Hollies Trout Farm, Sheldon, near Honiton. Tel: 01404 841428.

BEACHES

Beer
South-facing sheltered cove. Sloping pebble beach. Restrictions on dogs May–Sep.

Branscombe
National Trust. Faces south extending for 2 miles (3.2km). Pebble beach, sloping gently. No dogs on beach in front of café May–Sep.

Budleigh Salterton
Large pebbles/sandy. No dogs May–Sep in certain areas. Littleham Cove.

Exmouth
Flat, sandy beach. No dogs May–Sep. Sandy Bay: large sheltered sandy cove. No dogs mid-Jun to mid-Sep.

Otterton
Ladram Bay: small sheltered south-facing cove approached through the Ladram Bay Caravan Park. Shingle. No dogs Apr–Sep.

Salcombe Regis Village
One mile (1.6km) from Sidmouth. Sloping pebble beach. Park at church car park in Salcombe Regis. Dogs allowed.

Seaton
Spacious, gently sloping pebble beach, south facing. No dogs May–Sep between Castle Hill and River Axe.

Sidmouth

Jacobs Ladder: sheltered south-facing bay. Sand, pebbles. No dogs on beach opposite promenade May–Sep.
Town Beach: faces south, fairly well sheltered, sand, pebbles. No dogs May–20 Sep.
Weston Mouth: south facing, approached by footpath from Weston. Sloping, pebbles. Dogs allowed.

BOAT TRIPS

River, coastal and sea trips from Exmouth and Topsham. Stuart Line. Tel: 01395 279693. Also from Beer and Seaton. Details are available from local tourist information centres.

COUNTRY PARKS, FORESTS AND NATURE RESERVES

Ashclyst, near Exeter. Tel: 01392 832262.
Bullers Hill, near Exeter. Tel: 01392 832262.
Haldon Forest, near Exeter.
Otter Estuary. Public access by footpaths on either side of the estuary. Birdwatching.
Mamhead, off A380, near Exmouth. Tel: 01392 832262.
Stoke Woods, near Exeter. Tel: 01392 832262.

CYCLING

For information about cycle routes in the area – The Tarka Trail, West Devon Sticklepath Cycle Route, Mid Torridge Cycle Link and others – contact the local Tourist Information Centres. Also visit www.devon.gov.uk/tourism/ncn

CYCLE HIRE

Exeter
Saddles & Paddles, 14 The Cellars, The Quay. Tel: 01392 424241.
St David's Leisure Hire, Prestons Yard, Ludwell Lane. Tel: 01392 213141.
Exmouth
Knobblies, 107 Exeter Road. Tel: 01395 270182.
Honiton
Cycle Honiton, Lanson House, King Street. Tel: 01404 47211.
Sidmouth
Sidmouth Cycles, 110 High Street. Tel: 01395 579786.
W V Fish Cycles, 71 Temple Street. Tel: 01395 512185.

GOLF COURSES

Budleigh Salterton
East Devon Golf Club. Tel: 01395 443370.
Countess Wear
Exeter Golf & Country Club. Tel: 01392 874139.
Exeter
Northbrook Approach Golf Course, Topsham Road. Tel: 01392 667010.
Honiton
Honiton Golf Club, Middlehills. Tel: 01404 42943.
Sidmouth
Thorn Family Golf Centre, off A3052, east of Sidmouth. Tel: 01395 579564.
Woodbury
Woodbury Park Golf & Country Club. Tel: 01395 233382.

HORSE-RIDING

Budleigh Salterton
Budleigh Salterton Riding School, Dalditch Lane. Tel: 01395 442035.
Exeter
Haldon Riding Stables, Home Farm, Chideock nr Kennford. Tel: 01392 832645.
Honiton
Devenish Pitt Riding School, Farway. Tel: 01404 871355.

SAILING

Exeter
Haven Banks Outdoor Education Centre, 61 Haven Road. Tel: 01392 434668.
Exmouth
Spinnakers Sailing Centre, Little Shelly Beach. Tel: 01395 222551.
Seaton
Axe Yacht Club, Axe Harbour, Seaton. Tel: 01297 20779.

WATERSPORTS

Exmouth
Diver Training School, No. 5 Camperdown Terrace, Exmouth Harbour. Tel: 01395 266300.
Exmouth Windsurfing Centre, The Seafront. Tel: 01395 276599. Shop and school on seafront. Equipment for hire.

Annual Events and Customs

Axminster
Carnival, mid-September.
Exeter
Devon County Show, Exeter, mid-May.
Exeter Festival, late June to mid-July.
Honiton
Carnival, late October.
Ottery St Mary
Carnival, early November.
Jazz Festival at Cadhay, July.
Tar Barrel Rolling, 5 November.
Seaton
Carnival, early September.
Sidmouth
International Folk Festival, early August.

The checklists give details of just some of the facilities within the area covered by this guide. Further information can be obtained from Tourist Information Centres.

Bicton Park gardens have some exotic specimens among their collections of plants

Atlas and Map Symbols

THE NATIONAL GRID SYSTEM

The National Grid system covers Great Britain with an imaginary network of 100 kilometre grid squares. Each square is given a unique alphabetic reference as shown in the diagram. These squares are sub-divided into one hundred 10 kilometre squares, each numbered from 0 to 9 in an easterly (left to right) direction and northerly (upwards) direction from the bottom left corner. Each 10 km square is similarly sub-divided into one hundred 1 km squares.

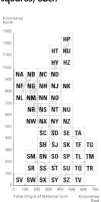

KEY TO ATLAS

⏧	Abbey, cathedral or priory	-----	National trail
⚓	Aquarium	NT	National Trust property
⚔	Castle	NTS	National Trust for Scotland property
⌒	Cave	🐾	Nature reserve
⚐	Country park	★	Other place of interest
🏏	County cricket ground	P+R	Park and Ride location
🐄	Farm or animal centre	♣	Picnic site
··········	Forest drive	🚂	Steam centre
❄	Garden	🎿	Ski slope natural
⛳	Golf course	🎿	Ski slope artifical
🏛	Historic house	🅸	Tourist Information Centre
🐎	Horse racing	·☼·	Viewpoint
🏁	Motor racing	🆅	Visitor or heritage centre
🏛	Museum	🦌	Zoological or wildlife collection
☎	AA telephone	░░░	Forest Park
⊕	Airport	·˙·˙·˙	Heritage coast
Ⓗ	Heliport		National Park (England & Wales)
🌾	Windmill		National Scenic Area (Scotland)

KEY TO ATLAS

MOTORWAY

═M4═	Motorway with number		A1123	Other A road single/dual carriageway
═🅂═ Fleet	Motorway service area		═════	Road tunnel
⚫①⚫	Motorway junction with and without number		─Toll─	Toll
❸	Restricted motorway junctions		▬▬▬	Road under construction
═❙═	Motorway and junction under construction		⬦	Roundabout

PRIMARY ROUTE

A ROAD

═A3═	Primary route single/dual carriageway		B2070	B road single/dual carriageway
═🅂═ Grantham North	Primary route service area		⬦	B road interchange junction
BATH	Primary route destinations		⬦	B road roundabout with adjoining unclassified road
⬦	Roundabout		⟶	Steep gradient
Y 5 Y	Distance in miles between symbols			Unclassified road single/dual carriageway
══════	Narrow Primary route with passing places		─○─✕─	Railway station and level crossing

B ROAD

KEY TO TOURS

🚗	Tour start point	Buckland Abbey	Highlighted point of interest
⟹	Direction of tour		
		─✕─	Featured tour
⊩⊩⊩	Optional detour		

KEY TO WALKS

Scale 1:25,000, 2½ inches to 1 mile, 4cm to 1 km

🚶	Start of walk		Line of walk
➤	Direction of walk	▷▷▷▷▷	Optional detour
	Buckland Abbey		Highlighted point of interest

ROADS AND PATHS

M1 or A6(M)	M1 or A6(M)	Motorway
A 31(T) or A35	A 31(T) or A35	Trunk or main road
B 3074	B 3074	Secondary road
A 35	A 35	Dual carriageway
		Road generally more than 4m wide
		Road generally less than 4m wide
		Other road, drive or track
		Path

Unfenced roads and tracks are shown by pecked lines

RAILWAYS

Multiple track	Standard gauge		Embankment
Single track			Tunnel
Narrow gauge			Road over; road under
Siding			Level crossing
Cutting			Station

PUBLIC RIGHTS OF WAY

Public rights of way may not be evident on the ground

Public paths	footpath	++++	Byway open to all traffic
	bridleway		Road used as a public path
Permissive path		◆ ◆	Named path
Permissive bridleway		Pennine Way	National trail or recreational path

The representation on this map of any other road, track or path is no evidence of the existence of a right of way

RELIEF

50 ·	Heights determined by	Ground survey
285		Air survey

Contours are at 5 and 10 metres vertical interval

SYMBOLS

▪	Place of worship	with tower	⊙W. Spr	Well, Spring
✝		with spire, minaret or dome		Gravel pit
+		without such additions		Other pit or quarry
▢	Building			Sand pit
▢	Important building			
· T; A; R	Telephone: public; AA; RAC			Refuse or slag heap
--□------ pylon pole	Electricity transmission line			County Boundary (England & Wales)
△	Triangulation pillar			
➤	Bus or coach station			Water
🗼 🗼	Lighthouse; beacon			Sand; sand & shingle
⌖	Site of antiquity			National Park boundary
NT	National Trust always open			Mud
FC	Forestry Commission			

DANGER AREA
Firing and test ranges in the area
Danger!
Observe warning notices

VEGETATION

Limits of vegetation are defined by positioning of the symbols but may be delineated also by pecks or dots

🌲 🌲	Coniferous trees	🌳 🌳	Non-coniferous trees
🌳 🌳	Orchard		Heath
🌿 🌿	Coppice		Marsh, reeds, saltings.

TOURIST AND LEISURE INFORMATION

⋀	Camp site	PC	Public convenience
🛈	Information centre	P	Parking
i	Information centre (seasonal)	☀	Viewpoint
🚐	Caravan site	⊕	Mountain rescue post
✕	Picnic site		

Index